STACK

An Introduction to the *Highest* Levels of Investing

Jeremiah J. Brown

CONTENTS

"Only when the tide goes out do you realize who's been swimming naked"

– WARREN BUFFET

INTRODUCTION

CAN ENDING POVERTY BEGIN ON PARK AVENUE?

Why, with so many educational resources at our disposal, do we *continue* to witness such a colossal global wealth disparity? Even more, how do we solve and combat this growing economic epidemic for good? I believe finding the solution can be as simple as visiting one strip of Park Avenue in New York City.

We often hear that the president of the United States is the most powerful person in the world, but when it comes time to raise money, our presidents go humbly to people who *really* have the power. Where do they go, you ask? The same place that our last three presidents all have gone to raise money for their campaigns, to the 700 block of Park Avenue. This illusive strip in New York houses the majority of the wealthiest people in the country. The upper crust of the one percent, the .01%. The 100 people inhabiting this small block radius possess more wealth than half our entire country, and they leverage this money to buy luxuries, experiences, and something more insidious, political control, the number one ingredient to controlling capitalism and rigging the game in one's favor. So it is almost ironic that just heading north on the same strip for ten minutes will reveal the effects of this outcome. On the other side of the Harlem river lies another Park Avenue, the South Bronx, home to the nation's poorest district, where one in four people live below the poverty line.

So, in today's America, where enormous wealth and political influence are synonymous, what are the chances that a person from the poor side of Park Avenue can get to the rich side? The more I dug into this, the more I realized how *stacked* the cards are against the little guy. There is one solution, and that is to read on. Let us start to study the strategic financial moves of this particular elite group and integrate these strategies with our passions and skills.

The goal of this book will be to:

Increase investing and financial literacy for everyone, and democratize market ownership.

Simplify the investing process.

Empower the ordinary person to invest like Warren Buffet.

Take advantage of the biggest commodity, information.

PREFACE

There seems to be a lot of smoke and mirrors in the world of finance and economics today. I understand that due to the proverbial 'language' of money and capitalism, many pragmatic and simple financial strategies, instruments, and opportunities are often left unseen, or simply missed, by the masses. So, my job in this book is to seep through the financial fog and unveil the hidden investment strategies in a way that is fully digestible and easy to understand. Throughout my series of books, including this one, you have the opportunity to get all the financial information taught in MBA programs and the homes of the wealthy in one place. From the introduction on how our monetary systems work, the fundamentals of the markets, gold and silver, to investments that are tucked away from ubiquitous mass media financial solutions, you will learn everything you need to begin or continue your journey to building and preserving your wealth.

But before I continue to inundate you with first class financial solutions, I first want to debunk the debate surrounding money and capitalism and its destructive properties. This concept that we hate rich people is a lie. We only hate rich people until *we ourselves* become rich. What we hate is a gamed system, a system rigged against our ability to compete on a level playing field. In the current system, fair play, access to capital, and free enterprise is dissected and manipulated through legislation and political control; these crony conveyances line the pockets of a few at the expense of many. In short, we do not hate winners; we hate cheaters.

Money is both the pulse and the root of any society. It doesn't matter if you are black, white, red, or blue; we are all affected by this one color: green. The number one cause of health issues is stress; the number one cause of stress is *money*. The number one cause of divorce: *money*. The lack of social mobility and opportunity stems from, you guessed it, the lack of *money*. Crime in any society can be traced back to the lack of opportunity, causing hopelessness. The culprit? The lack of resources including, well, *money*. Lack of education, theft, and many more ills of society, are also due to *money*, or the lack of it. I can go on and on. Simply put, the lack of education about money and capitalism has always been a problem within society. However, this same problem has become an opportunity for the wealthy, for the media, and for multinational businesses looking to profit off the 70% consumer spending within our society. These entities need to have one side of the population disinterested and uneducated about the highest levels of investing, because this capital allows them to spend and retain influence. That being said, welcome to a shift in the financial paradigm, where you will now have access to the same information that has been hidden in plain sight for decades. It is time to *stack*.

Chapter I:

THE SECRET TO GREAT INVESTING

Have you ever had the feeling that you were five, ten, twenty, or thirty years too late to do something? I know I have, especially when it comes to investing. I don't know about you, but listening to financial gurus and planners tell me that if I were to start investing at 10 years of age, I would have something close to 'one hundred billion dollars' keeps me in a constant state of panic and anxiety. One thing is for certain, my brain was not even fully developed at that age to know the value of time and money. Secondly, I am pretty sure that one's environment and affluence play a role in the ability to learn financial literacy that early. I hope you know where I am going with this. The point is, investing is not as black and white as the media tries to make it out to be. This statement holds true when it comes to the highest levels of investing, the hidden information that allows the ones invested in it sleep better at night. These investment strategies are often controversial or only applicable to the more 'sophisticated' investor pool. However, I believe we all have the ability to grasp these concepts, simply because these strategies are not rocket science. You don't need a crystal ball or a swami's hat to be an expert at all levels of investing. All you need is access to capital and to this information. Read on....

Willpower – STOP spending to reward yourself.

Look at what happened in the 80s, 90s, and 2000s: we witnessed an upscaling of the American dream. What used to be an aspiration for a comfortable middle class standard of living has today morphed into a widespread desire for affluent living. From desires of someday living in a mega mansion, to having your name on that prestigious Forbes list, the desire for a comfortable lifestyle has been exchanged for, well, the desire for *more*. However, the urge for spending in modern society has taken its toll on a psychological feature of ours called *will power*. Today, we are spending in order to keep up with the Joneses, not realizing that the Joneses are spending to keep up with the Gateses.

This competitive spending looks like this:

The *poor* spend to emulate the middle class.

⬇

The *middle class* spends to emulate the rich.

⬇

Today, *the rich* spends to emulate the Ultra Rich.

It is no coincidence that as average credit scores hit all-time highs, so have consumer debt loads. We are now living in an overspend culture, where equanimity is being trumped by the urge to outspend the next person. But why are we spending to compete, to appease our anxieties, or even to reward ourselves? Researchers from Stanford University found interesting data about willpower in relation to spending.

The study reveals that people mostly think of *willpower* when it comes to spending in two ways:

1. Something that is *unlimited* and will enable you to tap into it again and again.

Or

2. Something that is *finite* and requires a rush of energy and exertion.

People who believe in the second definition tend to lose money the quickest, whether that be through saving or investing. Whereas, the people who understand that will power is infinite and abundant tend to score the highest levels in emotional intelligence and demonstrate the ability to forgo instant gratification. The people who are in the second category subconsciously believe that forgoing instant gratification is not about saving and suffering. Rather, it is about forgoing the ordinary for the extraordinary. To do this often requires time, discipline, and persistence, and the people who are able to have the right amount of spending willpower tend to achieve their goals the quickest. In a way, willpower is a psychological action that helps you see what truly matters in the long run so that you can experience the unforgettable things in life. Never pity yourself if you are not rewarding yourself for your labor, accomplishments, or triumphs; instead, learn how to shift the mind into acting out of abundance rather than scarcity.

Save the Chicken!

Imagine struggling financially for almost half your life, only to get the opportunity to own the very last two chickens on earth. One male, one female. The chickens are worth approximately one million dollars together, but can also produce eggs. Yes, I can see the dollar signs rolling out of your eye sockets right now. I am pretty sure the thought of selling two chickens to access that one million-dollar payout would be enticing, right? The ability to sell these two exclusive chickens at a profit after being financial impaired might seem like a plausible and sensible solution, right? Possibly. What if I told you that it would be an imprudent financial strategy? You would probably think that I am crazy and incompetent, wouldn't you?

Selling the chickens might grant you that initial payout, winning the battle of a gain, but it would ultimately cost you the war of *cashflow*. A better strategy would be to sell the eggs these two chickens produce! This way, not only would you end up having the ability to monetize each egg produced, you would also be able to sell the chickens that grow from the eggs. This is why people in so many low-income communities get eradicated due to redevelopment and gentrification projects. The richest communities migrate into low income ones and play out their dreams of getting rich quick through real estate. The people within these low income communities, instead of monetizing the influx of wealth migration in perpetuity, sell their last 'chicken,' their asset. To make matters even worse, the thought of getting rich forces them to become flippers, overleveraging their debt loads and buying houses at inflated prices in hopes to sell to a bigger idiot. As the financial meltdowns ensue, and they always do, property values could plummet, and people in low-income areas will again lose everything. In my opinion, investing in real estate, stocks, or any other investment vehicle for capital gains is a Ponzi scheme. You are hoping that there is a bigger fool than you who will take on your financial nightmare. I don't know about you, but if I am not able to predict the future or deceive someone, then it is challenging to make profit speculating.

> *"Buy your 'toys' like clothes, cars, and vacation homes off profits of profits, and never spend the principal. Build profits, and then enjoy the cash flow you receive from them.But never, ever spend the principal."*
>
> *—Kevin O'Leary*

The true way to be liquid asset rich is to invest in real estate, stocks, or any other investment vehicle for cash flow. Converting your ordinary income into passive income is as simple as following this strategy.

In doing so, you will begin to see both your income and assets expand exponentially over time.

Where is my ROI?

"It might NOT be prudent to have 80% of your net worth tied to one stock called your home."

—*Jeremiah Brown*

Before we delve into the secret to *great* investing, I first want to address what investing is and isn't. Investing, whether with stocks, real estate, businesses, or people, is simply a belief that the market currently underprices an asset. The value is what the *investor* expects will eventually rise significantly, whether it be its price, brand, intellectual property, or the returns from its profit. The investor, in other words, decides to act on something that the market has missed or is missing. This seems simple, right? Well, many people forget one more important component to investing. That is the *ROI*, or return on investment. We are often caught up in the next best thing—that new cryptocurrency, the most recent IPO, that new business idea, a tax regulation change, a new hit single, and more—that we forget that the ultimate goal is to get a return on our investment capital. These returns can either be in the form of cashflow, my favorite type of return, or capital gains (profit), but they should never look like a wish or a lottery.

To really make money with any investment, you have to invest with this notion in mind. Since interest rates are at an all-time low today (which means that multiples in any investment will be higher, due to people rushing to get a yield, or a return, on their money), you will pay higher premiums on investments. This seems good if you are a speculator looking to buy and flip, hoping to find a greater fool. However, in the event that rates begin to rise, prices will fall, and you will be left holding the bag if you speculated at the wrong time. This is why fundamental investing, or investing for cash flow rather than through flipping, is a sound strategy in any economy and market. Capital gains should always be the icing on the cake.

"Hope is not a strategy"

—Vince Lombardi

Buy $10 bills for $5

Price and value are *not* the same thing. Price is what you pay for something, but value is what you get. For example: if you pay 200k for a 120k Bentley, you still just have a 120k Bentley. In this scenario, you would have gone into the purchase at an 80k loss. The worst thing you can do in buying anything is to *overpay* for it. The same rules apply with investing. In stocks, the market price may not represent the true value of a share. Many times, it is its book value or intrinsic value that displays how much the stock will be worth in the event of a liquidation. The same holds true in real estate investing. Here's an example. If an investment property is listed at $250,000 and the appraised value is $200,000, buying it at its list price forces you to spend an extra $50,000 on the property, money that could have otherwise been used to add value to the property and increase its price. You want to make sure that there is upside in any investment that you purchase, otherwise you will be paying to wait. Paying to wait just to get into an investment is not a great investment philosophy and can hurt any first time investor who does not plan to hold the investment forever.

The worst thing you can do in any investment, whether it be with stocks, real estate, or businesses, is to overpay. It does not matter what you buy; you just have to know what you are buying and how much it is truly worth. When it comes to investing, profits are made when you *buy*,

not when you sell. A buyer's success in any deal is heavily dependent on this fundamental rule. You can always go up, or buy at the height, but what separates the savvy investors from the masses is their ability to buy low, or spot a deal and opportunity.

Where is my 30% discount at Louis Vuitton?

If you are interested in getting a deal from luxury retailers, you must learn to see what the financially uneducated are blinded by and find discounts for assets rather than liabilities. Whenever I hear of a company like *LVMH* having an in-store sale, I immediately check its stock price to see if the company itself is 'on sale' and trading at a discount. Unfortunately, the poor mentality tells us to shop for liabilities that are on sale. Bargain hunting like the rich by buying assets that are on sale should be a part of everyone's financial strategy. This is a proven way to increase your wealth and build your income stream so that you can buy liabilities on sale with the profits from your acquired assets. This technique is how you amass a real fortune within our society.

The majority of information and financial advice consistently perpetrated by the media and finance industry is absolutely wrong. This is because there are two types of financial information in this world:

1. Financial information for the **99%**
2. Financial information for the ***1%***

Imagine Ferrari or Lamborghini having a 75% sale. Would you not be inclined to buy the car before the sale ends and the price returns back to its original MSRP? Well, this is the same buying strategy that the wealthy get from their financial insiders. The .01% buy stocks, real estate, businesses, and now cryptocurrency when *nobody wants them.* The information given to the rich has little to do with financial data and more to do with behavioral finance and human psychology. There is a reason why many of the top economists responsible for running our monetary system never even studied finance. Instead, many earned their credentials in the field of psychology. The financial information provided within the elite club is to buy assets when they're hated, when people are selling in fear, when there is "blood in the streets." And when is this the case? You guessed it: during bad economies and economic downturns. Instead of reacting to the media as it pertains to financial information, get your shopping list ready like the rich and get ready for a pullback. Then, buy "cash flowing" assets on sale so that you get paid while you wait.

Many of us however, only shop for liabilities that are considered on sale, such as a nice car, exclusive sneakers, clothes, and jewelry. Although these items make us poorer and cost us money in the long run, we convince ourselves that this is the right way to bargain hunt and "save money." However, the wealthy approach bargain shopping completely differently from that of the financially uneducated. The rich wait for pullbacks in the stock market and corrections in real estate and purchase these assets "on sale" as the herd begins to sell in fear. The rich also invest in assets such as businesses, gold and silver, and technologies that will be at the forefront in the future before people are made aware of it. This is how they are able to sleep and have their money make more of itself for them.

Your Money is Bored

There is a ubiquitous phrase floating around Wall Street: "money never sleeps." Although there is some truth to this metaphor, what you're not told is that money often gets bored. Once your money becomes bored with stagnation, whether in savings or idle investment vehicles, it will go searching for a vacation, a car, entertainment, or problems to keep itself busy. When you accumulate money, your primary goal should be to get rid of it as fast as you can. Now, I am not saying that you should recklessly depart from your capital, or even spend it on consumables like an expensive bag or on entertainment. What you should do is look for investments that will keep your money busy. You should never just 'sit' on money. Money is useless in today's economic climate if it is not being converted to cashflow.

"If investing is entertaining, and you're having fun, you're probably not investing, but gambling."

—Jeremiah J. Brown

Sure, there was a time when all you had to do to grow your money was to leave it alone in an interest bearing savings account or in your house where you live. There was even a time when you were guaranteed a consistent paycheck as a result of a city job or sitting in a cubicle for 48% of your entire lifespan. But today, when the world is changing around you and money is becoming digitized debt causing boom and bust cycles in perpetuity, it has become extremely difficult to gain wealth, let alone stay ahead of your money. Tie this in with outdated financial information and rhetoric that contradicts an ever changing monetary environment that we are a part of, and you have a population of debtors working for money, only to have their money disappear into the debt loads that they accumulated in the first place from traps disguised as "advice." This is an outdated financial strategy that keeps us on a spinning wheel of chasing a dollar controlled by the dollar creators. It is quite easy to keep pushing that dollar up as you struggle more and more to catch it on that economic wheel you call opportunity.

Money moves faster than a Lamborghini

Have you ever driven a Lamborghini? If you haven't, imagine having 700 thoroughbred race horses pass you all at once. The amount of force produced by these illustrious creatures would have you gasping for air as they passed. Just as fast as they would be in your peripheral vision, they would be in your rear view, leaving you guessing how they were even next to you during that ordeal. This is the same pace at which money travels. Today, the speed of producing data, information, and services has gone up to extreme levels unseen by generations of the past. However, one of the reasons why there has always been a huge wealth disparity between the upper class and the middle and lower class has to do with the *velocity of money*. Many invest their money in the following ways:

- Through saving and dumping money into the house that they own and occupy.
- Using stagnant investment vehicles like 401ks, 529 plans, or pension plans.

The wealthy, however, do the following:

- Acquire assets using *leverage* (or OPM).
- Pull their initial investment out of those assets, without selling the assets.
- Buy more assets with that same money, rather than park it and retire their money as the poor and middle class do.

The wealthy investor keeps his money moving and increases his velocity of investing. So you should understand why your money hates being stagnant. Income that you retire into investments typically requires a capital gains tax once it is time to sell. When the wealthy invest their money via debt or *OPM*, they can use the same cash and increase their asset column tax-free, because it is debt-based capital at work. The wealthy can acquire assets, like real estate, which pays them cash flow from renting out the units. Then, through a refinance loan or a home equity loan, they receive their initial capital back and repeat the steps all over again, decreasing their tax liability, and increasing the velocity of their wealth and income.

- **Question: *How do I find good investments in this low interest rate economy?***

Stocks:

In this environment, companies can easily artificially inflate their earnings within their earnings reports by leveraging borrowed cash (or debt) and buying other companies with it. They don't have to reinvest the money back into the company on property, plant, employees, or equipment for real intrinsic growth. These companies can simply acquire other companies, lay off workers and show that their earnings have increased, even with antiquated technology or business models. It is the equivalent to an athlete using steroids, as opposed to working out naturally in order to get their gains. So, my criteria for finding a good stock has little to do with a company's earnings report, especially in a low interest rate environment.

Here is how I sort through the hype surrounding a stock and analyze a great company (outside of reading its 10-K statements). I look at it very simply. The first thing I look at is GDP growth. This is the rising tide of any economy, and it determines the macro-economic state of businesses. I then find companies that have growing free cash flow. In other words, the company has to display free cash flowing in after capital expenditures. If you always look at the free cash flow of any investment, it will keep you safe and confident. Simple deals that have an understandable business model and an easy path to revenue are the keys to financial abundance in investing.

Through MSN money or Morningstar, I find companies that I know have strong economic MOATS (or competitive advantages). Once I've identified the company's stock, my analysis consists of finding the following criteria:

- ***Income statement**: Summary on how any company incurs (or gets) its revenue and expenses.*
    - ➤ <u>Goal</u>: Net *Income* should always be **POSITIVE**
- ***Balance sheet**: Shows a company's assets vs. its liabilities and the difference is called net equity.*

➤ Goal: Net *Equity* should always be **POSITIVE**

- ***Cash flow statement***:

    - *Operating net cash flow*: **POSITIVE**

How much money the company is generating every year. Obviously, the goal is to see a positive number here.

- *Investment activities*: **NEGATIVE**

This number represents the company investing back into the company. *Negative* means the company is reinvesting capital gains back into itself.

- *Financing activities*: **NEGATIVE**

You want the company to either buy back their shares, increase the stock price, or distribute dividends to the shareholders.

I then check analyst ratings and their analysis of a stock. In my assessment, I am looking for the following:

Price to earnings: *Determines if the stock or company is overvalued.*

My strategy: No more than 18 times the company's annual earnings

Price to book: *Determines the real value or book value of the stock or company.*

My strategy: No more than 2 times book value is the ideal number

Debt to equity ratio: *Measures the riskiness of a company, and its vigilant leadership by comparing its debt to the amount of equity it has.*

My strategy: Ratios at .40 or lower are considered ideal metrics.

Current ratio: *Determines whether or not the company's liquid assets are greater than its liabilities.*

My strategy: 1.5 above; this means that assets are at least twice as big as liabilities.

Here are other, more advanced metrics to consider:

- **Margin of safety** = Book Value/Share price (Closer the equity is to the market price, the safer the investment).
- **Competitive advantage** or **Economic MOAT**: The gross profit margin shows the economic viability and MOAT of a company. The higher the margin, the more of a dominance the company has in its particular industry.
- **Gross profit margin:** Inspecting the gross profit margin is where you determine the MOAT of a company:

Gross profit margin assessment:

35% and under = LOW DOMINANCE

35% - %50 = MEDIUM DOMINANCE

50% or more = HIGH DOMINANCE

As in real estate, the numbers and economic dominance both play a major role in your decision to buy a piece of any business. Remember, stock is simply a piece of a business. You, as the shareholder, share in the risk and rewards of a company. But, with the introduction of derivatives and bundle investment vehicles (*401k, mutual & index funds, REITs, ETFs, CDs*) no wonder people are not able to excel in investing like Warren Buffet. Focus, block out the noise, and commit to your strategy.

Where is my profit?

One thing I enjoy about this strategy is that you can see through the lies of any company or investment. There is no vision, there is no pitch on how this new company will revolutionize the world, but your money is needed in order to do it, there is just *cashflow*. This is the only thing I listen to when it comes to making an investment in any asset class outside of physical gold and silver (which are only insurance policies on fiat currency). The money coming in should be the only story you should see and hear. This, I believe, is the secret to great investing. Why is this my philosophy? Simple. I've lost money more times speculating than I have making a sound fundamental analysis on a company. It is interesting that, when it comes to investing, my pessimism has earned me more money than my reckless optimism in speculating. In any investment, you should have a tiny element of fear. You should assume that whatever you are investing in, whether it be stocks, bonds, businesses, or especially commodities, there is some probability that you will lose it all. It could hit zero, which is why you always need to have a reserve, some cash set aside so that, if everything fails, you are still okay. This is the same pessimism that you should have in analyzing an investment opportunity.

Options (only if you like to speculate)

If you think stocks have reached their peak and you are afraid to jump in and invest, looking for stocks that are overvalued "shorting" them or buying inverse ETFs to protect your portfolio from downside risk can be the remedy that you need to relieve your fear and skepticism. There will always be stocks that are ready to move higher or lower, regardless of any bull or bear market run. Learning how to profit from downward movement is just as important as profiting from the rallies within the stock market. You will never be late to the investment party if you understand this simple strategy. Instead of doing what the masses are taught to do, which is to jump in when the market is rallying and run away to sell when there is a pullback or collapse, doing the opposite will give you the significant gains you need to survive any market you are in. Remember, it is not stocks that will make you rich; it is knowledge along with timing that will.

"The risk of an individual home is just as volatile as the stock market"

—CEO of Unison

Note: *Using a stock screener will allow you to input these numbers in weeding out the speculative stocks from the ones really producing profits and returning free cash. The key to life is the check coming in. It's the only thing that I look for in any investment strategy and so should you. If a company fails to meet the above criteria, it will be extremely challenging for me to invest in it. The money would have to be money that I would normally gamble with at the casino, and the investment would be a whimsical one. The cash flow from any investment will be the only thing that will has the potential to be certainty in your life. It will be the only friend, equality, security, or cute pet you're going to have when your old and wrinkled. Listening to popular financial advice from CNBC and the like will manipulate us to invest in the next IPO, crypto, or biotech company that we know nothing about. This is not investing. This is called buying the hype. I am only helping you spot the difference.*

You will need to understand how you can use the liquidity you have to buy assets, whether it be in stocks, exchange traded funds, real estate, or bonds that appreciate and pay you while you wait. The truth is we all can make money, but only a few of us can reach financial freedom and wealth through sound and poised investing. Arriving at this plateau takes not only knowledge but a burning desire to become free from economic deprivation and the ability to see and leverage both sides of the economic coin (income and debt).

Quick Tip: Before getting into investing, whether you are investing in stocks, bonds, real estate, or any other investment, the first step you must take is planning. Financial planning serves as your roadmap and is critical to the outcome of your financial goals. Before you begin your journey of legacy investing, you should ask yourself the following questions:

- What are your financial goals?
  - o Will you be investing for the short term, long term, or investing for generations understanding the possibility that you may never reap the benefits of your investment with the generation strategy?
- What is your risk tolerance?
  - o Are you risk adverse or risk tolerant? Always remember: returns rise with risk. This means the more risk an investment may have, the better the potential for a high return.
- Do *you* want to actively manage your portfolio?
  - o If you would like to manage a portfolio yourself, education and time management are key elements in the success of your investments. The more you educate yourself and the more time you allocate towards investing, the more successful you may be. If you'd like to have your portfolio managed on your behalf, education and time management is key. Just giving your portfolio to a professional to manage it does not guarantee success. You still must understand what they are investing in and why they are recommending what they are offering you. Sometimes this initiative requires that you manage your time wisely to allocate time to review and audit your portfolio managers and advisors.
- How should I diversify?

- Simple! Don't put all your eggs in one basket! I am pretty sure I don't need to elaborate on this one.

You want to be extremely careful speculating in today's economic climate. Many investors today are jumping into riskier assets in order to find a desired return. It is pretty interesting to see how everyone is trying to find anything of value right now. I believe, by suppressing interest so low for so long, we are seeing a mass flood into bad and speculative investments. Investors and fund managers are desperate to find anything that generates a yield and fights against inflation. It is quite puzzling that, although this has been the greatest time to build wealth in America, the greatest fear today is not dying poor, it is living poor. The only remedy that would alleviate this fear would be to invest for cash flow and focus on value first, then profit, in any investment.

If money doesn't grow on trees, then why do banks have branches?

Chapter 2:

LEVERAGE THE BANKS

It is important to know that the banks' number one function in business is to make money on our money. Simply put, they are designed to monetized the debts of both people and businesses. Nothing more, nothing less. Banks take a portion of your savings in order to lend it out to other people, reserving a fraction of your savings in their vaults. They then collect profits on the *spread* between what other people are paying in interest and what they owe you in interest. This process is known as fractional reserve banking. In fact, 92–96 percent of all currency in existence is created by our banks! Only 3–5 percent of all currency is created by our government. If you want to know where and how to get money, the answer is located in any bank or credit union in America. The bank is simply valuable if you are leveraging their financial relationship or keeping your capital in it to pay your monthly bills and other immediate expenses. However, when it comes to anything else, including your emergency fund, your money should be parked elsewhere! I am going to reveal why.

"Keep your money close and the banks even closer"

— Jeremiah J. Brown

Be friends with the bank

There is nothing more important in business or finance than your relationship with the bank. The bank has all of the money and they are willing to share as much as 80% (or more, in most cases) with you, if you develop a special kind of friendship with them. The benefit of working with the bank is that they put up most of the money but only want the interest on the money they give you. You give up no equity, and you have full control over what you want to do with the asset. This is a much better option on a cash producing asset than bringing in partners in exchange for equity and control. The banks aren't in the business of operations; they are simply lending money to make money on what they lend. The only way to develop a friendship with the bank is to have what the bank wants and needs. The banks funding mindset is rather idiosyncratic. They either fund people and businesses who theoretically don't need the capital, or they fund deals that generate cash flow and offer the underlying asset as collateral. Simple. All the bank really cares about is money in and money out.

For example:

- ➤ If you have a simple functioning, often non-tech, business, like a dry cleaning business, that earns roughly $100,000 per year, you can walk into a bank and they will give you a line of credit and other business loans.
- ➤ If you bring them a good deal on a commercial property along with 20-35% of your own money (depending on the deal), in most cases, they don't even care to inspect your credit, as long as the deal is profitable and you can prove it or your income.

The truth is, the more loans the bank gives out, the more money the banks make. That is the primary business model of these financial institutions, and if you understand it, the banks will be at your mercy. Banking is the key to everything and the more you borrow from them and repay them, the better leverage and rates you will get from them in the future.

If you are thinking about parking your money in a bank, giving the bank permission to invest and lend out your money, you want your money to grow, correct? In order to determine how quickly it would grow, you would need to follow a financial formula called the rule of 72. Here's how the rule of 72 works; you will divide the number 72 by the interest rate you will receive (say 1% or .01), and the answer will be the number of years it would take for your investment or capital to double in value.

- Divide the rates by 72 in order to see how long it will take your money to double:

YOU

Interest rate	**Years to double**	Account
0.01	7200	Your Savings Account
0.035	2057	CD
0.25	288	Standard Bank IRA

- Now let's compare that to the length it takes banks to make a return:

BANK

Interest rate	**Years to double**	Loans
4.14%	17	Auto Loan
5.50%	13	Mortgage rates
22.99%	3	Credit Cards (*bad credit*)

That is how the whole machine works. It is a simple but brilliant system on their end. It is not necessarily beneficial for you as the saver. So, it is easy to see why many people share in this love-hate relationship with banks. But banks, my friend, have all the money and need to dispense it to continue their and the country's economic survival. And, like that awkward person at school or work, the banks can really be your friend if you take the time to understand them.

> *"All the bank really cares about is money in and money out."*
>
> —Jeremiah J. Brown

It is frustrating enough to know that banks only need you when you have money and don't need them, but with the lowest interest suppression in history requiring a low return on savings, how can anyone agree that banks are your friend? The answer is as simple as generating tangible assets or showing them a good deal that they can use as collateral against your down payment.

Leverage the 'relationship' with banks to become the bank

When leveraging the bank's money, you want to make sure that you have sufficient credit (620 minimum), and save up as much as you can to support a down payment. Believe it or not, banks take the most risk in a real estate deal. How? Think about it. They will loan you money to buy a property, and they will loan you money to fix it up through what is known as a 203k loan. A typical FHA deal requires you to only put down 3.5%, while the bank is responsible for covering the other 96-97% of the deal. In other words, for every $100,000 on a deal, you would only have to cover $3,500! How often have you spent $3500 in any given year on things you don't really need? Think about this the next time you receive a big payday or save up. The way to beat the banks is to first be friends with the bank. The bank is your friend if you understand how to leverage the relationship.

If you ask your financial advisor or banker what a good return on your money should be, odds are they will show you an antiquated and ubiquitous chart showing you historic and theoretical data of returns ranging from 7-10%. These numbers represent industry expectations and returns that a retail investor should have after investing money into the stock market or real estate.

To put it in layman's terms, using simple numbers:

You put up **$1000** dollars.

⬇

You will get a 7% return (**$70** return on your money).

⬇

Your ***money*** is still required in order to make this $70 return.

In this model, you would need to have your capital invested into the asset in order for the asset to produce money for you. With this strategy, it would take a long period of time in order to not only recoup your initial investment, but to profit from it entirely. You are not using the power of leverage effectively.

What if I told you that, once again, the information you've been given in regard to money is not all true. Fortunately, for many of us, seeking a 10% yield is considered to be "short change" compared to the strategy I am about to reveal. By leveraging our 'friendship' with the banks, we have the ability not only to make money out of nothing, but also to produce income in perpetuity. This process is called producing an *infinite return*. The definition of an infinite return is simple: owning a cash flow producing asset with no money invested into the underlying asset. This is an advanced technique that holds benefits far beyond just a return on your ideas or creative financing.

Whether you are interested in owning a single family home or a commercial property, the same rules to creating an infinite return apply:

- Buy the asset using the bank's money (75% Loan-to-Value).
- Take out your initial investment either through a refinance or HELOC.
- Allow the cash flow from the property to pay off the debt and produce a profit for you.

Here is an illustration of the infinite return production strategy (I will use simple numbers to make it easy to understand):

You invest: ***$1000***
Initial Cash-on-cash return: ***limited***

⬇

Use power of leverage to get your ***$1000*** *back*
New Cash-on-cash return: ***Infinite***
(Because your 'principal' is no longer being invested)

Caution: Real estate is a very finance- and management-intensive proposition. You have to know your numbers in order to achieve an infinite return in this space. The good news is, it does not require complex math or formulaic equations. You only need simple addition, subtraction, and attention to detail in order to excel with this strategy. Let me simplify it for you: don't let your eye off the profit. Producing an *infinite return* simply means that you are taking back the cost to own the property and getting cash flow as well. It is a 'both and' scenario.

What if the bank rejects my friendship?

In many cases, especially in real estate, when you lack 'things' that the bank wants to continue the financial friendship, you can find ordinary people to assume the role of the bank. If you lack sufficient credit or are unemployed but have a lump sum of cash, you can still acquire property through the following strategies.

1. You could go through an option known as *seller financing*. This is where the seller acts as the bank, and you pay the seller a mortgage instead of paying the bank. You still own the title, but the seller has a lien against the title until the mortgage is paid off (the same as if you went through the bank). This benefits the seller because the seller isn't subjected to the hefty capital gains tax and can collect a fixed income and charge interests, as opposed to having a one-time lump sum that would be taxed. I only recommend that you do this if the property is owned free and clear (paid off—which 30 percent of all homes in the United States are). This is because if the sellers have the mortgage with the bank and if you miss any payments or if the seller does not pay back the mortgage, the bank can technically foreclose on the property, leaving both you and the seller out of a property.

2. You can find homeowners who are struggling to pay their mortgage and who are in default. These are called NOD's or notice of default documents (*ask a local agent in your area for the list*). You offer to relieve them of their financial burden by proposing to pay the back payments that they owe on their mortgage and give them extra cash in their pocket in exchange for the owner to deed you the home.

An example would look like this:

- Owner owns a property at $200,000.
- The owner has paid to date $100,000 toward the principal of the property. However, due to a job loss or economic hardship, the owner owes $15,000 on the property, and as a result of not paying it, he is in default. This is when you step in.
- You offer owner $30,000, which would cover the owner's debt and put cash back into his pocket, in exchange for him transferring the title or deed to you. If the owner agrees, you now own a $200,000 home for $30,000, and you have instant

equity of $85,000, which includes the original $100,000 the owner paid down on the mortgage, minus the $15,000 that you paid toward the owner's debt.

This is an advanced strategy, and I recommend that you consult your real estate agent and ask them to send you their *notice of default* (NOD) forms. You may also want to seek out an attorney for more information. But this is another creative strategy to get into the real estate game.

The bank's partnership criteria

Finding out what the bank wants in a partner is as simple as asking. Go to a bank and ask what the money and credit requirements would be to secure a partnership with them. Ten times out of ten, the bank will let you know exactly what is needed to leverage their cash and partner with them. The banks absolutely love real estate and simple cash flowing deals like a laundromat business or a franchise. To banks, real estate offers a nice simple business model. You get someone a place to live, they pay you the rent, you pay all the bills with the rent, and whatever is left over is *yours* to keep. The banks profit off the financing they provide and the mortgage you owe. The fact that real estate has the ability to pay you while you wait for said property to appreciate in value is exactly the investment needed to combat inflationary or deflationary events and volatility in any economic cycle. Even in a low interest rate environment, where asset prices inflate in order to adjust to the amount of currency pumped into the economy, there are still ways to make a profit in real estate. This is why banks are in love partnering with you in real estate. You assume the responsibility, workload, and risk, and they just put up the money. In most cases, your personal credit score isn't a requirement in their decision to loan you money. In most cases, all you need bring to the table is the 25% and a good deal. The banks love good deals and numbers: understand this, and the banks will be at your mercy forever.

See, banks aren't so bad after all, huh?

***Question:** Do banks not care about your credit score when you are buying a property?*

Honestly, when you make it to a level where you want to do commercial banking, the current assets that you own will become your new credit score. The banks may run a quick credit check just for giggles, but it is primarily the money and the assets that determine your fate in partnering with the banks on a commercial deal. The banks want to know whether you are financially capable of supporting the commercial deal, and cash or your portfolio would play a major role in the bank's decision to go in on your deal. It is very important to have a good credit score and, no judgments, but you want to focus on acquiring assets that produce positive cash flow to show the bank that you know what you're doing.

Banks love it when you STACK

Why do you think banks love it when you save and stack your money with them? It is simply so they can leverage your money to make more money. In order to build that pristine relationship with the banks, you must use their trick against them. Have you ever heard of the saying, "The worse you treat them, the more they like you?" This could not be more accurate than with the banks. Leveraging their money to make more money is how the banks will begin to love and respect you. We have been conditioned throughout financial media to leave our economic energy called *money* to the banks, not knowing the goal is to have them leave their money with us! My job in introducing you to the highest levels of investing is to unveil the information that the wealthy and super wealth are using. The same information, ironically, has reinforced a negative undertone to building wealth using OPM. The more you understand this financial strategy, the more financially independent and knowledgeable you will become. Leverage the bank's money (not in your name, but with an LLC) to make more money and build wealth for yourself.

We really own nothing

I know most of you are wonder why, if we could simply use other avenues in order to create or generate cash flow for ourselves even in real estate, do we need banks so much in society? The truth is, the banks are, for better or worse, the cornerstone of our economic system. There is absolutely no getting around the banks, and even if you use seller financing or print your own money legally, you will eventually need to go back to the banks for certain transactions. When it comes to real estate, you are either renting from landlord or renting from the bank via a mortgage. If you do not have a mortgage and own a property outright, you are paying property taxes on it in perpetuity. When you die, the property goes back to the state or to family members who will sell it and probably waste the money. In the end, you really own nothing in this world. However, the banks own one thing and one thing only; capital. The more capital they own, the more they are willing to deploy it, and the more you can transfer that capital ownership from them to you. Think about it….

"Money never declines. Money just moves."

— Dick Kovacevich

Chapter 3:

FORTUNE FAVORES THE GOLD

"Gold is money, everything else is credit."

—J.P Morgan, 1912

In my 29th year on the planet, I decided to take a trip to where it all began: Africa. While in the motherland, I stopped in Cairo, Egypt, for a short visit. Egypt is such an enchanted place, as it reveals some of the most mysterious monolithic structures, artifacts, and meridian energy on the planet. Although these discoveries were fascinating, there was something more eminent that was uncovered: the origin of money. Roughly 5000 years ago, the Egyptians started using gold and silver as their form of currency. But these precious metals were not yet considered money and that was because of a few things:

1. *The units of gold and silver were not interchangeable like our dollars today. They were odd sizes, different weights and purities, and they could not technically put an exact price on any*

good or service. In simple terms, it was still a guessing game to determine the true value of something.

2. *These precious metals were also not as portable then as currency and digital money are today.*

However, the reason that gold and silver have always been the optimum form of money is because of their properties. For one, they are *limited in quantity*, preventing government and central banks from printing them or manipulating them, as they could fiat currency (Dollar, Pound, Yuan, etc.). Pure gold, unlike currency, has the same *store of value* anywhere around the world. One ounce of gold can buy the same amount in Egypt as it would in the United States, India, Russia, or China. It is *durable* and has proven its durability, because the same gold that the Egyptians used 5,000 years ago is the same gold that has been melted and reused today. The use of gold has evolved over the years, from the Egyptians sculpting big tomb blocks out of it, to countries breaking it up into smaller *divisible* units of account. As a result, Gold has become just as portable as the dollar itself, although still underlying digital money like credit cards.

Honest money

People are amazed that, after more than 5000 years, the pyramids are still with us today. What impresses me more is the fact that the currency of the people that built those pyramids is still here and being used today! I believe that is the definition of honest money. The reason gold and silver are called *honest money* is that they have maintained and preserved their value for millennia. For anything to be considered money, it has to maintain its purchasing power for a long period of time. Unlike gold, since the inception of the Federal Reserve in 1913, our Dollar has lost over 97% of its purchasing power. An example of this would be to look at real estate or—you guessed it—the price of gold. You can see an inverse correlation between our currency and gold and real estate. Overtime, as the Dollar has decreased in value, gold and real estate have increased. This is because assets, like gold and real estate, soak up an expanding currency like a sponge does water. The more the U.S. Fed prints dollars or lowers rates, the higher asset prices climb. The relationship between gold and debt-backed currency is similar to a check and balance system.

Up to today, there have been thousands of rulers and thousands of fiat currencies like our Dollar, many unbacked by gold and silver. And they all have gone to zero. Yes, every single fiat currency ever to exist in any nation has gone to zero or printed to oblivion. The truth is, debt backed currencies have a 100% failure rate and that is because of one thing; the loss of 'confidence' in the ability to pay back astronomical debts overtime. Yes, it is a confidence game that our currency is playing.

"Gold is the ultimate form of money, and nothing is in the same league. I understand why it's been classed as a commodity and not a currency. You can maintain a solvent and sovereign system because of gold's global use. It has a global dominance."

—Unknown

The GOLD bull run has begun

Why are people interested in buying negative yield bonds today or investing in equity markets with overvalued valuations (prices)? Why has there been an urgency to 1031 one's real estate profits into deals that don't make sense over the last couple of years? Why this sudden rush into lousy deals? Simply put, people are looking for safe haven assets. This search for yield and safe assets have now become a global issue. Central banks everywhere have accumulated massive amounts of debt that their citizens are responsible for. So, more and more, people are going to invest in gold as a hedge against this global increase in debt.

If you want exposure to gold in your investment portfolio, simply buy gold itself and forget the mining stocks and the derivatives of gold. I personally like gold because it is a stabilizer and an insurance policy on our debt-based currency. Although it probably sounds like it, I am not a doomsday preparer, nor do I care about the possibility of any hyper-inflation or depression happening anytime in the future. What I use gold for is simply its ability to store wealth. It is the only asset that I own that does not pay me to wait. There is a reason why countries own it and why it is classed as a commodity.

How to buy gold and silver

Okay, enough with the education on precious metals. How do you buy *gold and silver*?

The first thing that is needed is, well, an education on how to buy correctly. There are two types of precious metals:

1. ***Physical Bars***: (Gold, Silver, Platinum, Palladium bars)
2. ***Paper / Derivatives***: (Gold & Silver *ETFs*)

In the case of physical bars, the units of measurements are the same, whether it be in platinum, silver, gold or palladium. Let's, for the purpose of this demonstration, talk about buying a standard gold and silver bar. There are different sizes or weights of these bars, and these weights vary in price according to size. Let us take a look at the weights.

There weights are measured in:

- ***GRAMS***
- ***TROY OUNCES***

- ***KILOGRAMS***

So depending on what you can afford, the weights will substantially determine the amount of gold and silver bars you are able to buy. In the stock market, paper gold and silver (ETFs) are only measured in ounces, so you can only buy at the price per ounce. However, with physical bars, you can buy bars in smaller quantities than ounces, like in grams.

Time to buy: the last step

At this level of understanding, you are now able to start the buying process. To begin the process in purchasing your precious metal, the first step will be to look up an accredited gold and silver coin store in your area—make sure they are registered and have reliable reviews—and head to the store. One thing to look out for when you are buying a physical bar is something known to many precious metal investors as a 'spot price.' Spot prices for gold and silver may vary based on the coin store. A *spot price* is simply the premium that you pay for purchasing that asset. In layman's terms, it is the store's profit or *spread* for selling you that precious metal. Everyone has to make a profit; it is a business, at the end of the day. Your job as in investor is to make sure you get the cheapest spot price possible, because you are going to pay spot. From my experience buying and selling gold bars, a spot price under $2 is ideal. The price may be different for you depending on many different factors. However, the industry barometer of a $2 spot is something to base your purchase decision on. Once you see how much the store's spot price is, it will be up to you to decided what the weight of the bar will be. I would keep it simple; I would stick with buying one-ounce gold and silver bars and hold them.

Note: *Similar to car brands, the price of gold and silver bars are also priced by the brand that they were refine from. For example, a reputable brand is the PAMP, ROYAL CANADIAN MINT 1oz GOLD MAPLE LEAF, Credit Suisse and others. Another determiner of price will be quality. I advise you to shop only for gold and silver bars that come in a package* *and never take it out of the original package. This ensures the sustainability of quality and the authenticity of the bar.*

The Ultimate Strategy

Whenever you are getting into the game of investing, whether it be in stocks, bonds, real estate, or in this case physical gold and silver, the strategy should always be a long term one. Buy and hold forever and don't increase the position of any one asset past 20% of your portfolio. This doesn't mean that you should *never* sell; I understand that life happens, and you may have to liquidate assets at some point in time. What I am simply saying is you should never go into any investment playing a hot potato financial game, where you hope to flip and sell it at a higher price than you bought it at in an extremely short period of time. With regard to precious metals, I would keep a 5% weight in precious metals in my overall portfolio, which means that I would only have 5% of my money tied to gold and silver. I don't care if gold climbs up to $40,000/oz, I'll be selling on the strengths (bull run), and will be buying on the weak (dips in the price). It is simple. This is a strategy that I mentioned during my segment on Fox and Cheddar. Why? Gold is simply a hedge against inflation. If anything happens to our economy, whether it be a down market, economic downtown, hyperinflation, or deflationary event, gold will always be the default currency and insurance on a debt driven economy.

Question #1:

Which investment offers better store of value? Gold or Bitcoin?

Cryptocurrency—Bitcoin, in particular—is merely a digital derivative of physical gold, in my opinion. Why? Just pay attention to its nickname: *digital gold.* Its purpose was to add another economic store of value, this time digital, and defense against a corrupt monetary system, i.e. our current debt-based currency. However, upon its conception,

Bitcoin was widely used as a monetary shield for terrorists, tax evaders, money launderers, and other criminal activity. Cryptocurrency is still very new and has not yet weathered a financial crisis as gold has. That is a big uncertainty right there; leaving aside all of the issues of its volatility, criminal use, and other negative implications, we have absolutely no idea how Bitcoin will perform in an economic panic.

Gold, however, was here before humanity and will be here even after humanity ceases to exist. It has been a consistent and proven barometer of any fiat currency to have ever existed, and like real estate, is a hedge against inflation. There is a reason why the price of gold has increased as more currency has been printed. There is a limited supply of gold and silver and it is widely utilized in almost everything we use in modern society today. This is why not adding physical gold and silver could be like not getting life insurance on your money. The choice is yours.

Question #2:

Which is safer? Gold or Bitcoin?

The fact that it is unregulated is why I am actually concerned about Bitcoin. This leaves Bitcoin and other cryptocurrencies vulnerable to one of the oldest scams in the book: the pump and dump. What industry insiders, or people with a ton of money, could do to pocket profits at the expense of the financially uninformed and speculators is "paint the tape." This means that market manipulators could simply increase activity in the price, but only by trading the cryptocurrency back and forth. This would look like my buying Bitcoin at $10,000 and selling it to my brother for $11,000. He then sells it back to me at $12,000, and we repeat the steps again and again. We just traded the same crypto back and forth, there was no P&L that Bitcoin reported, no earnings beat, or dividend payout that helped increase its overall market value. It is simply activity due to speculation and market price manipulation. But the point is, this brings in the suckers, or the financially uneducated to leverage their house to 'invest' in this rapidly growing investment. Always remember, subjective value has always trumped real value. And subjective value when it comes to buying Bitcoin over gold is simply a liquidity preference. So, I look at these two economic stores of value as a liquidity preference more than I do an outright competition.

The only way you can manipulate gold is to either do it through its paper form (gold ETFs) or by debasing the metals or adding copper elements to gold. Then again, you could make a case like this for every single form of money ever created. What I like about gold is its economic resistant properties, as explained earlier. Gold and silver both serve as insurance policies on our debt-based monetary system. These precious metals regulate inflation, which is an expansion of fiat currency, and have historically risen in unsound economic times. The best part, in my opinion, is the potential. Since they are regulated as commodities rather than currencies, gold has artificially been compressed. This means that gold has been sitting on the sidelines since 1971 when Nixon detached gold from the dollar. Remember, all currency before 1971 was a claims check, or a receipt for gold. That mean that a $20 bill was a representation of real money which was $20 worth of gold. But when gold was taken off, hard assets began to accelerate in value over-time. This means that once gold is financially recognized, you will see its true trade value. Does Bitcoin's price ring a bell? That's what once ounce of gold is really worth.

Chapter 4:

THE IRS HAS ITS FAVORITES

The tax law, once an equal opportunity income taker, has now become nothing but a series of incentives for entrepreneurs, investors, and owners who understand and take full advantage of it. In the United States alone, more than 80% of the tax code is used to stimulate economic activity relating to business, agriculture, real estate, and energy. Following the code correctly in any of these economic verticals will continue spearheading the largest tax disparity in history. No wonder the working class shares a similar morbid sentiment about the tax code. However, tax planning should be a part of everyone's wealth strategy. Why? Because it is not what you make that often matters, but what you keep and continue to keep. When you keep taxes in mind whenever you're investing, you will end up keeping more of your principle and make better decisions.

90% of the tax code is written to benefit entrepreneurs and investors.

—Provision Wealth

Decipher the tax code

Let's dive right into it. There are two types of capital gains:

Short term capital gains (one year or less hold)

&

Long term capital gains (more than one year hold)

Short term capital gains are taxed at your personal tax rate. If you are in the 35% tax bracket, you will be taxed at that 35% rate on your short term cap gains. However, if you hold onto the asset for more than a year, you qualify for long term capital gains. This allows for a lower tax base, usually 15 -20% on your gains. Rudimentary stuff.

Now, the way our American capitalist system is set up, it is specifically and strategically designed for owners and investors to succeed. Allow me to give you a personal example: when I sold my property in Las Vegas, I paid nothing in taxes. *Zero*! Why? Well, simple:

1. I just deferred the gains using a tax vehicle known as the 1031. This vehicle allowed me to skip paying taxes as long as I used the gains from the sold property to buy a property equivalent or greater in price. With this move, I was able to save thousands in taxes and still get access to my money. Now, here is the hack to getting my money out of an investment without losing it.

2. Once I acquired another property, I refinanced after about five months and was able to get out 80% of my money, which accounted for my original investment plus some of the profits, all tax free. I wish this was taught in school, but I was able to learn this through investing and owning. Investing and owning is the income for the rich. Ordinary income, like from a job, side gig, or being self-employed, is and will always be the poor and middle class's income. It will

also always be taxed at the highest rates. If you have both incomes, you are still winning; but always remind yourself that your portfolio and passive income will always be taxed at lower rates than your physical labor. I hope you see why the word "freedom" is in financial freedom.

Why is debt the solution to avoiding the *IRS*?

Ever since the Federal Reserve's printing press began in 1971, the dollar has lost more than 90 percent of its purchasing power. The US Dollar will continue to lose value due to the effects of the big bank bail-outs, trade wars, keeping interest rates low for a vast amount of time, and quantitative easing. Every dollar in existence is owed back with interest, so the more we print, the higher our taxes are, and the more expensive assets become due to inflation from currency printing. Now you see why it makes more sense to learn how to use debt to acquire assets that provide cash flow. This is why financial education is now more important than ever before. Instead of spending your entire life saving and working for money, you can leverage good debt to increase your wealth financially. People take on debt to seek education and buy liabilities, but very few people believe in the principle of utilizing debt capital (that tenants are paying for) to avoid paying taxes. This is why becoming financially educated can give you a competitive edge in the inevitable shift to globalization.

Question: *Isn't using debt to buy real estate assets risky?*

Answer: Not as risky as using your credit card (debt) to buy liabilities, like a pair of $500 Louis Vuitton shoes, groceries, or even your bills. The game that we are all in is about "who owes who," so if you are leveraging debt to acquire assets that someone else is paying for and what is left over is profit for you, then you are ahead of the game!

1031 tax deferral: worth more dead than alive

Basically, the only way to win in a 1031 exchange is to die. Why? It brings the taxes that you deferred over the years to what is known as a step-up-basis. Let's say you purchased a property worth one million dollars and, after two years or so, it climbs to $1.5 million. If you sell, you would have to pay capital gains on the profit: $500,000 of the 1.5 million. However, if you use what is known as a 1031 exchange, you can pay no taxes only as long as you immediately (45 days, 6 months to close) go out and buy a property worth $1.5 million or more. Insane, isn't it?

Now here is how you win in a 1031 exchange. You can roll the profits into another deal and take it out of that deal utilizing a refinance. This is where you get up to 80% of your money out of the property tax-free, because it is debt capital at work. This capital has to be repaid, but as long as you have tenants, it will be. Enjoy your tax free profits and roll it over to another deal to grow. See, the beauty in real estate, when it comes to defending you against the IRS, is that as long as you stay in the game of leveraging 1031 tax deferment, you are protected. It's the equivalate to becoming a 'made man' in the mob. Yes, that is right: the IRS is the financial equivalent to the mafia, and as long as you leverage the 1031 or opportunity fund, you are a 'made man' or woman. You are, in a way, forced to grow your portfolio and invest in bigger and bigger deals in the long run. The only caveat is, like all gangs, you are only protected as long as you are in it, and the only way out is to, well, die.

Tax hack for the ordinary person

It is safe to say that, although real estate has become a popular investment in today's climate, many people do not have the stomach or aptitude to be the next Robert Kiyosaki. Most people would simply like to make decent living and live comfortably. I can certainly argue with that, and I am pretty sure Robert Kiyosaki can as well. But, even if you are not a real estate tycoon, you can still benefit from these tax incentives without having to monitor a 1000-unit portfolio all the time. For those wanting to live well and capitalize on the tax benefits of owning real estate, here is a simple hack for you to save money on taxes on your owner occupied dwelling:

1. Buy the cheapest house in the nicest neighborhood, whether that be a foreclosure, fixer upper, or short sale.
2. Fix it up using a 203k loan.
3. Live in it for a minimum of two years.
4. *Sell it*, and as long as you live in there for exactly 24 months (2 years), you don't have to pay any taxes on the gains. If you are single, that means no taxes on gains up to 250k. If you are married, your gains are tax-free up to 500k in profit.
5. Rinse and repeat.

Whatever you can do to make the property better while you sit on it for two years, you should do it. Whether it be subtle upgrades, or an entire rehab job, these options contribute to the *value added* component in real estate. You can even spend a little bit of money to spruce up your property to make it look nicer in order to charge extra: using cheap pieces of granite slabs, adding stadium lighting, crown moldings, paint, and changing only the doors and knobs of cabinets. These are all creative ways to increase the value of the property in the tens of thousands, without spending tens of thousands of dollars.

You CAN touch the 'sacred' cow

If you are a first-time homebuyer, have not owned a home for the last two years, and have a Roth IRA, this is the wealth hack for you. You can take up to $10,000 from your Roth IRA, free of penalty, to purchase your first home. Since a $10,000-per-person withdrawal is allowed without an early withdrawal penalty when used to buy your first house, you are allowed to access the cash and use it toward a down payment on a home. It gets better: you are even allowed to use this tax-free IRA money to contribute to the down payment for a spouse, parent, and child. This is a great way to ensure that you leave a legacy for your children and family.

401k tax hack

The 401k program has historically been the go-to investment for the retail investor looking to conservatively save and invest for retirement. If you voluntarily enroll in a 401k plan, theoretically, its goal is to force you to save for retirement. Based on historical data, 401ks have returned anywhere from 4-6% over the average investor's life—an okay number if you are open to giving up control of your finances to someone else, hoping that they will do a better job then you. If this is the case, then the 401k investment vehicle may be an ideal option for you, right? Let's take a look. According to *Fidelity Investments*, more people have earned over a million dollars in 401k accounts than ever before, with 196,000 accounts totaling one million dollars! Sounds great, right? Not so fast. Let's look at the real numbers:

- *There are* ***60 million total*** people enrolled in a 401k plan.
- Out of the 60 million people enrolled, ***only 196,000*** 401k accounts are at $1 million by the age of retirement.
- ***Less than 1%*** of the population have made $1 million in a 401k by the age of retirement.
- ***The median balance*** of an average 401k account ***by the age of 65 is $64,811.***

Yes, *$64,811* is the real number if you consider all 60 million people invested in a 401k. This number is heartbreaking, considering how many people work 40% of their lives and sacrifice putting most of their earned income into a 401k, only to have a few years off work after retirement. They run out of money due to the 401k savings depletion and are forced to go back to work at 70 years of age, working at Walmart to survive.

Side note: Still not convinced? Okay, if you can show me one person who has become a millionaire in their 20s from a 401k, you can close this book now. I will wait.... You can't. Why? That 20-something 401k millionaire can't exist because of two reasons:

1. *Time* and *math* won't allow it.

2. The *government* won't allow it (due to annual contribution limits).

The old mantra in relation to employment investing says, if you access your 401k before your retirement, you will be taxed to the moon and back. The bearer of this information is either uniformed or misleading the masses. On the contrary, you can access *your* money from your 401k, and you can do it tax free. Welcome to the 401k tax hack, where as long as you invest the money into another performing asset, you can leverage your 401k capital to make even more capital. *Here is how it works:*

- You *borrow* from your 401k up to 50k (or up to 50% of your total amount).

- You then pay *yourself* back with a *market based* interest (say, 4%).

Please keep in mind that there is probably an 18-month period before you can do this again.

The benefit is that you are paying yourself back as the lender, then benefiting from the cash-flow from your performing asset. By borrowing from your 401k, you are essentially becoming your own bank, while paying yourself back with interest. In other words, you are keeping all of your money and leveraging it at the same time. It's a win-win—but likely something mainstream financial media wouldn't reveal.

Opportunity is in your zone

An idea was originally discovered by Senator Timothy Scott and technology entrepreneur Sean Parker, along with other billionaire founders, to avoid paying capital gains tax on their billion-dollar profits; it has turned into a huge opportunity for everyone looking to build wealth, contribute to the economic enhancement of society, and avoid paying taxes while doing it. Welcome to the Opportunity Zone. We could argue whether this initiative will have negative long term effects (gentrification) on the very communities that they stand to help, but that is another topic for another day. What I will do today is show you how you can also get in the game and invest in this opportunity.

If you decide to sell any asset (*whether it be a business, stock, property, or even crypto-currencies*), and experience gains from that asset, normally you would incur a tax bill for those gains. Today, with the introduction of Opportunity Zones, as long as you sell your assets and roll the gains over into an Opportunity fund or zone for development, you will incur no taxes on the investment after ten years. Yes, you heard correctly: investors can enjoy a permanent exclusion from taxable income of capital gains from the sale or exchange of an investment in an Opportunity Fund, should the initial investment be held for at least ten years. Any hold less than ten years would require you to pay some taxes, but at a significant discount to what you would have had to pay, if you didn't convert the gains into an Opportunity Fund or Zone.

Here is a detailed layout of the tax:

- **Fewer than 5 years**: Deferred payment of existing capital gains until the date that the Opportunity Fund investment is sold or exchanged.
- **5 – 7 years**: The above benefits and 10% of tax on existing capital gain is canceled.
- **7 – 10 years**: Deferred payment of existing capital gains until December 31, 2026, or the date that the Opportunity Fund

investment is sold or exchanged (whichever comes first) and 15 percent of tax on existing capital gain is canceled.

- **Greater than 10 years**: The benefits of the 7 – 10 year investment and investors pay no capital gains tax on the Opportunity Fund investment.

Opportunity Funds allow investors throughout the United States to utilize their untapped resources and park it into tax friendly Opportunity Zone investments. This strategy is considered to be a 1031 on steroids.

The IRS has its favorites, too

With many of the special incentive programs out there for businesses and real estate, it is safe to say that the IRS favors corporations over individuals. Knowing this, I do not own anything in my name, just as the rich do not. My assets are held in my C corporations, LLC, and trust. If I stumble into a lawsuit from someone looking to make a quick buck, I will not have anything to give personally. Creating a corporation allows one to avoid the two biggest monetary predators in the world which are:

- *The government (IRS)*: taxes
- ***People***: lawsuits from people who want to sue you for their mistakes

If you want to pay less in taxes and have more asset protection, don't change your mentality from wanting everything in your name to protecting your castle by putting your assets under your corporation.

Tax and income protection

Due to a law passed in 1943 (*Current Tax Payment Act*), if you are an employee of a company, the money you earn from your paycheck is immediately taxed. Have you ever noticed how your stated salary is different than what you take home every year?

- ➤ *For example*: Your salary says $50,000, but you take home $26,500 after taxes.

Well, that is due to this act, which was passed before you and I were even born. Through the Current Tax Payment Act, you are taxed the entire amount of your salary, as opposed to being taxed on what is left over after you pay to live. What makes this immediate taxation worse is that you have to live off the $26,500, not the $50,000. You earn, then you're taxed, and then you can spend what is left over—in that order.

If you pass your income through your corporation, then you can expense your earnings *before* the government taxes it.

It looks like this:

- ➤ You earn, you spend, and then the government gets to tax what is left over, if there is anything left over at all after your write-offs. (For example, I earn $50,000 through my corporation; I expense or spend $46,000 of that $50,000; and I am taxed only on the remaining $4,000, not the $50,000, which I would have been taxed on if I worked for a paycheck.)

This has been a common focus of the wealthy as they pursue and maintain their wealth.

Cheating death taxes?

People often ask me if they can give money away without being taxed. The answer is YES! If you are fortunate enough to have more than $675,000, or $5 million, but want to escape the estate tax upon death, then I have the perfect solution for you! If you have not heard of a loophole known as the unified tax credit, I advise you to pay attention to what I am about to reveal. This, I believe, could possibly be an estate tax loophole commonly used and practiced among the elite but kept out of popular financial planning and advice for the masses.

You can make gifts of $14,000 or more per year to any of your children or grandchildren. That's right! You can gift as many people as you'd like $14,000 or more per year. Now, here is the kicker. Remember the exemption amount is up to $675,000, so if you have an estate less than this amount, you can gift it all without being taxed on any of the amount given. There are even some cases where you can gift up to $5.75 million through this exclusion, and not be taxed federally at all! This loophole is called the unified tax credit and is one of the many strategies used among the wealthy to avoid the estate tax.

The only thing to look out for are the taxes the inheritor will have to pay on any *gains* that are incurred by the beneficiary. In other words, if you give your child $50,000, and your child invests this money and makes an extra $8,000, your child will only be subjected to pay taxes on the $8,000. There is no step-up in basis, which is beyond the scope of this topic. However, it would be worse if the beneficiary inherits your estate after you pass on. The inheritor of the estate, or beneficiary, would still pay taxes on any profit or gain from the principal, and, unlike the unified credit, the estate would even be taxed. Double taxation vs. no taxes; which would you choose?

Pay no taxes whatsoever

Today, a company can simply move its assets, IP, and other forms of profit transfers on paper. These maneuvers allow a company to escape the 35% tax base and increase revenue and net profits. No wonder Apple Corporation has close to $400 million trapped overseas tax-free. Your job is to do as Apple does if you want to profit at the same rate as Apple has.

What if I told you that there are *new tax havens* outside the traditional states like Delaware, Nevada, and Wyoming, which some of the most popular American corporations use in order to hide over $60 billion a year? This type of cryptic information is hidden from the popular financial experts and media by mega-corporations as well as small mom-and-pop companies looking to save on taxes as well. Do you believe this corporate phenomenon is happening? Well, one major way they avoid paying the tax man is by parking their profits overseas. With a 35% tax rate and a tax code encouraging offshoring, who would blame these corporations from hiding money in the Cayman Islands and Bermuda, Switzerland, or Ireland, where there are no taxes at all. Thanks to effective lobbying and savvy lawyers, you have the ability, within the parameters of your company, to exploit the provisions within the tax law. In fact, every other government applauds lowering their corporate tax base to rates that are attractive to many US companies, and that is why these US corporations go there. But why can't your business go there? It's because the information is hidden from you. Whether you are offshoring, creating corporations, or setting up strategies like the ones mentioned above, what you are essentially doing is finding loopholes to preserve your money and assets.

Unfortunately, due to people taking advantage of these secretive protections, the term *loophole* has had a negative connotation within our society. However, it really comes from the idea of how you protect yourself. The word *loophole* was derived from the holes in castles during the Medieval time period, when people would sneak through and shoot arrows at their enemies through the holes in their castle. Today, the loopholes are set up so you can protect yourself from anyone trying to attack your wealth or the fruits of your labor. Because Vikings in the form of taxes, lawsuits, and bad debt could at any time attempt to attack your investments. The beginning and end goal of your efforts in building wealth and increasing your passive income should be to protect your assets like the rich.

The three richest people in the world have a greater wealth than the bottom 50%

Chapter 5:

THE MASS MIGRATION OF MONEY

In my lifetime, I am sure we will witness the biggest wealth transfer in the history of our economy. Why? Central banks all over the world are playing with fire by printing boat loads of cheap money. Our money is now becoming toxic as a result. The more toxic our money becomes, the wider the gap between the haves and the have nots become. Today, the markets keep going up and up, with zero interest rates, and that is what keeps pushing it. Tie this with tax havens for the rich—like the carried interest loophole, which allows hedge fund managers the luxury to pay less taxes than his secretary, and non-repatriation, which forces companies domiciled in America to earn trillions of dollars overseas and keep the profits there. These are the ingredients of a wealth transfer.

Throughout history, printed money has never worked, from the Romans debasing their currency in 250 AD, to the death of the continental dollar from hyperinflation in 1776. It seems that every time a monetary system runs out of money, the only solution has always been to create derivatives of money. So what do you think our country will do? Stop spending? My take is that they will take a play out of the old history books and create derivatives of money, which in this case is debt-backed currency. In order to understand why this change is happening and how our monetary systems let this happen, one must understand the history of money leading up to today. Policy changes that happened within our monetary system over 30, 40, even 100 years ago still affect us today. *Let's see how*:

1913

⬇

Inception of the **Federal Reserve** (*signed into Congress by a Democrat through what was known as the Glass/Owen bill*) can create money out of nothing and pay it back through, well, you!

1913

⬇

Introduction of the ***Income Tax*** (coincidence?)

1944

⬇

Bretton Woods Agreement: Since the United States owned the world's largest *gold* reserves, an agreement was made to have every currency in the world be tied to the US Dollar.

1971

⬇

Nixon takes the dollar off of the gold standard: Money becomes fiat, or backed by debt. The income distribution begins to move in very dramatic ways towards inequality, with the top 10% of the population's wealth and income increasing by 40% over the following years.

2009

⬇

Following the largest market crash since the Great Depression, **corporations owned by the .01%, are bailed out and given a stimulus** in hopes that it would trickle down to the masses. The corporations used most of it to give out large bonuses to top executives and to buy back their shares, increasing the stock price, and making themselves further rich.

2010 -?

⬇

Longest interest rate suppression in history: Within the past ten years, there has been a lowering of interest rates, with fiat currency being backed by no real intangible asset outside of a promise to pay it back through taxing incomes. According to many economists, this has been the longest period of interest rate *suppression* in over 5000 years!

"Tax dollars are needed for the Federal Reserve to create more dollars."

- *Robert Kiyosaki*

This inevitable collapse has been proven throughout the history of our monetary existence dating back to the Continental Dollar. Fiat currency has been replaced many times and will probably continue. What does not collapse, however, happens to be the economy behind the currency. It will not matter if there is another great depression or great recession, there are everyday and ubiquitous things that people will need in order to live. *Procter & Gamble* is a company that owns everyday goods, services, and appliances that we use, even during the recent recession. Assets that provide housing, food, transportation, and even education will always be in demand. Just find the assets you think are recession proof and return cash back to you and invest. This is how you protect yourself.

With all of the monetary changes that have happened in the past and happen today, I wonder how the next 100 years will look due to the monetary decisions of today? Whatever the outcome may be, the upper class will continue to learn the game, master it, and identify how the

Federal Reserve can be their ally. The more the Fed continues to print currency, the more assets they will leverage via debt, and, as a result, the less taxes they will have to pay. My advice? Play the game, learn the language of capitalism, and have fun doing it! Because the game will not change, unless the institutions that constructed this insidious game ceases to exist.

Are you "liquid asset" poor?

I want to take this time to highlight the homeless. Why? Because there has been a de-humanizing stigma for quite some time now regarding their social economic situation. Homeless people have been dismissed as 'lazy, mentally ill' people, and outright forgotten. This narrative has commonly stemmed from the late 1980s, when Ronald Regan cut federal funding for shelters housing the mentally ill, flooding the streets with them and creating an influx of homeless mentally ill people over time. Seems like a fair argument. But what if I told you that their inability to earn an income is not the reason why they are homeless. Would you agree? Sure, earning an income is an important part of the equation. However, the inability to weather financial hardship can set anyone on the path to homelessness.

> *"Two thirds of the population are a paycheck away from homelessness."*
>
> -CNBC

According to an article published by the personal finance site, Bankrate, "Just 39% of Americans say they have enough savings to cover a $1,000 emergency room visit or car repair." That means that the remaining 61% of the total U.S population don't have at least $1000 in savings. Contrary to what is shown through the media or social media, the majority of Americans are technically broke and one paycheck away from homelessness.

Today, it seems that having liquidity or cash flow is now more important than ever. Whether that be from earned income, cash from leveraging good debt, or other streams, controlling where your money goes and the consistency with which it comes in is the new way to determine your financial health. Sure, the ubiquitous and socially accepted *net worth* tends to be a great barometer of your financial scorecard or performance. However, net worth only acknowledges your good habits from the bad ones. It fails to accurately detect how economically liquid you really are or aren't in the event of an emergency. This is why not only do you need to have a reserve set aside; you also need to garner a diverse array of income streams. How? It's as simple as reading on…

How to spot a potential economic slowdown

I am pretty sure many of us get our financial news from mainstream media, magazines, or maybe even through YouTube's financial sensationalist. It seems that every time the market is down for a period of time, there are aggressive headlines pointing to a recession or worse, an outright economic disaster. There has always been evidence pointing to warning signs before any economic downturn. From the 2008 real estate bubble, the early 2000s dot com bubble, all the way to the Great Depression in the 1930s and tulip mania back in the 1600s, macro-bubbles have always inflated due to market panic, irrational exuberance, and government and central bank negligence. How are people able to determine when the warning signs are beginning? And even more, how can investors capitalize or increase their wealth during the next one?

The writing is on the wall sort of speak. Or in this case, the credit wall…

		Rating Type	
Number	*Moody's*	*Standard & Poor's*	*Fitch Ratings*
1	Aaa	AAA	AAA
2	Aa1	AA+	AA+
3	Aa2	AA	AA
4	Aa3	AA-	AA-
5	A1	A+	A+
6	A2	A	A
7	A3	A-	A-
8	Baa1	BBB+	BBB+
9	Baa2	BBB	BBB
10	Baa3	BBB-	BBB-
11	Ba1	BB+	BB+
12	Ba2	BB	BB
13	Ba3	BB-	BB-
14	B1	B+	B+
15	B2	B	B
16	B3	B-	B-
17	Caa1	CCC+	CCC+
18	Caa2	CCC	CCC
19	Caa3	CCC-	CCC-
20	Ca	CC	CC
21	C	C	C
22	-	D	DDD
23		SD	DD
24		-	D

**This chart shows the credit agents and their risk ratings measuring the credit worthiness of a company.*

This chart shows the credit agents and their risk ratings measuring the credit worthiness of a typical company. What I started noticing during these economic slowdowns were a ton of mass market businesses, including large retailers with revenues ranging from $100 million to $20 billion in revenue, being downgraded. Companies like J.C Penney, Toys R Us, Pier 1, David's Bridal, Forever 21, and others, would go from a 9 risk rating to an 18 risk rating. The higher the number, the worse it is for a company, and the more likely it is for a company to go bankrupt because of too much debt. In the 2008 bubble, paying attention to news surrounding the economic crisis, I started noticing a high credit risk ripple effect across industries and sectors, with layoffs quickly following. Banks and financial insiders quickly spotted this trend, realizing that major companies were reducing their workforce by 20-35% within a short period of time. What followed after was the straw that broke the camel's back: the loan defaults. Although this example was applied to the housing crisis, these indicators have always been used as a measuring stock of a pending financial calamity underway.

Most Fortunes are made during a recession

My ultimate prediction is that the next recession will not be like the bubbles of the past. You know: when cops and teachers making about $50,000 were qualified for mansions that cost more than $1 million dollars, and a pin-prick of mortgage defaults exploded an entire housing bubble. Instead, the next economic contraction or recession will be long and slow. This is because the central banks have been pumping artificial money through lowering interest rates, reducing reserve requirements in banks to the lowest in decades, and continuously printing money. Although there will be similar economic indicators as in the past, this amount of Federal Reserve 'generosity' has never happened before. Thus, the results will be unlike anything we've ever experienced before.

With that being said, many fortunes have been made from investors capitalizing off the monetary negligence of our leaders. In fact, John D. Rockefeller, an American oil tycoon who built one of the largest and most eminent oil company in the history of big business and is one of the top 10 richest people of all time, stated this about how to make money in a recession or depression: "*The real way to make money is to buy when blood is running in the streets.*" You can imagine why I am focusing on economic downturns as a way to get rich and build wealth. Now, allow me to share with you my strategies on how I approach investing going into a down economy. I am sure you've heard in sports that the best offense is defense. I am also pretty sure you've heard before that the best defense is an even better offense. My strategy consists of two components:

- ***Defensive strategy***
- ***Offensive strategy***

My defensive strategy may seem like common sense to many of you reading. But always remember, when it comes to money and investing behavior, common sense is *not always* common practice. Let's continue.

My defensive approach would be the following:

1. **Pay off any *high interest* debts**: In any economic downturn, having high interest debt would be the equivalent to a death by 1,000 cuts. You know, those high monthly recurring payments from buying stuff that you don't want or need to impress the people who don't really care about you. These payments will drain you and sink your financial ship if you lose a job or have a drought during a recession. The goal here will be to tackle this high interest *consumer* debt first, before talking debt you can control or manage.

2. ***STACK* your capital:** Similarly to the title if the book you are currently reading, the next focus should be to create a reserve of capital. In other words, if have no dependents relying on your income, you should be saving at least six months equivalent to your rent and have that in cash. If you are the sole breadwinner or work in an unstable industry, you should have at least six to twelve months of savings. If you are retired and living on a fixed income, you should have saved at least five years of savings in reserve. These options, although they are applicable to different ages, are for the event that you want to take advantage of opportunities in the market, or even to stay afloat and ride some of the hard times. Now, I am not saying saving will be easy, or maybe it will: the goal is to simply get in the mindset of taxing yourself first in order to save.

3. **Maintain your *equanimity:*** If you already have positions in the market, or money tied up in business or real estate, do not *PANIC* and sell! The worst thing you could do is try and catch a falling knife. Even in 2008, when much of the

market lost almost 45% of its total value, it rebounded back and even doubled in value over time. In that time, a monkey throwing darts at a dart board could have made money on the rebound, so don't panic and give the opportunity to someone who understands that the price has nothing to do with the fundamentals of the asset. The most important thing for any investment is not to overpay and over leverage.

So, now that you have all of the defensive strategies to help you brace for a financial crisis impact, let's talk about how you can capitalize in a down market utilizing the offensive strategies that I am about to share.

My offensive approach would be the following:

1. **Diversify your *financial* castle**: With this approach, you should be diversifying your asset class. This financial castle should consist of *cash, gold and silver*, liquid assets like *money market accounts,* and *dividend paying stocks*. You want to have as much liquidity or free cash as possible in order to capitalize on pull backs in the market or worse, an outright downturn. If you picked up a bunch of rental properties in 2008 or invested in stocks traded at a discount, you would have tripled your money in value and earned positive cash flow along the way. Most fortunes are made during recessions because of this type of preparation.

2. **Invest in *stages* and *automate***: Never, I repeat, never buy all at once. The reality is, no one, not even Warren Buffet (unless he causes it), can determine when a pull back or a recession will happen in the market. This is why systematic investing, or *dollar cost averaging* down (which enables you to buy at regular intervals), is a tool used by the best traders to hedge their bets against a stock going lower or higher. The goal is to end up being somewhere in the middle or low end of a stock pullback and capitalizing off its bull run, without having to make any volatile predictions. You can do

the same in real estate, although the language would appear differently. Homes that go into foreclosure can be purchased by you at a discount, and you can immediately cash flow the property, until the prices normalize.

3. **Own your economic *MOAT*:** The best way to survive in difficult financial times is to develop a strong economic moat. Having a monopoly or expertise on information, whether that be a particular elusive skillset, or knowledge, will serve as your economic ticket when times are tough. It will not matter if there is a recession or economic slowdown, people will still need to laugh, learn, be entertained, eat, sleep, and do many other things that they can't live without. If you have unique skillsets, or have a competitive advantage, you will always have the ability to eat and feed your family in any market. When the goal is to sustain, you start out providing a service using your moat; but eventually the goal is to become an owner of other moats to alleviate your workload and buy back your time.

In my opinion, since many of the world's currency is tied back to our US Dollar (through the Bretton woods agreement of 1944), this massive form of printing and interest rate suppression has become a global issue. Today, a correction is imminent due to global inflation running rampant and valuations in the markets at an all-time high. In this country, we always overdo everything. If low interest rates boost the economy, keep it lower for longer. If corporations can leverage cheap money to buy back stock instead of investing in its people, they'll keep doing it. If the credit card, mortgage, or car note payment is low, more people will just keep spending and getting themselves deeper and deeper in debt. This behavior is a part of a never ending cycle, and cycles always revert back. So whether a recession will happen or not, the purpose of this defense/offense strategy will be to ensure that you are financially prepared to take advantage of any boom and bust economic cycles.

"To turn $100 into $110 is work. To turn 100 million into $110 million is inevitable."

— Edgar Bronfman, Jr.

Chapter 6:

HIGHEST LEVELS OF INVESTING

All investors can learn from what the wealthiest do. Whatever the size of your investments, the basic strategies should be similar. The number one goal for the ultra-wealthy is to buy back their time. They tend to focus not on the amount of money they can make, but on the number of days they can survive without physically working. Wealth in their eyes is measured in time, not dollars. Many of us, however, trade away moments of our time, day by day, year by year, for money, just to spend it on items that require us to work more to maintain them. These liabilities force us to trade more of our time to make up for the money lost. This repetitive cycle of trading time for money puts us in a never-ending rat race, coercing us to chase something that always seems to get away from us. This consumption philosophy will end after this chapter, if it hasn't already. This is because I am going to reveal investment strategies that allow you to generate a "set it and forget it" income generator. Ready?

Owning capital is the gateway to wealth

If you ask a billionaire what is the worst part about being one, chances are that billionaire would say "nothing at all." To a billionaire (worth approximately 3 billion dollars), large ticket items that an average person considers expensive are merely novelties. Want an example? Buying an island, for a billionaire, would be like an average American earning $50,000 a year and putting a down payment on a $200,000 house. Buying a $200k Bentley to a billionaire is like an average American spending $50 on groceries from their nearest supermarket. Let's put it this way: if all of the billionaires today formed a country, it would be the eighth richest country in the world. The term money is a little different for a billionaire.

"Money is too valuable to spend."

—billionaire unknown

The common trait that I discovered in all billionaires, no matter the industry they are in, is that they all owned capital. The richer you are, the less your money comes in from labor, and the more it comes from capital. In fact, more than 70% of their earned income derives from their capital. It is almost the complete opposite for an average employee earning a salary, with 75% of their income coming from their labor. Want to know why the rich get richer? They own capital and get taxed less for doing so!

But what is capital? Capital is simply anything you own that can produce an income for you. An example of capital would be the following:

- Owning à an investment property
- Owning à stocks
- Owning à intellectual property
- Owning à businesses
- Owning à your likeness or popularity

- Owning à patents, trademarks, copyrights

Owning Capital allows you to do thinks like:

- Rent out what you own
- License it (*having someone pay to use the name of your asset*)
- Sell it for more than your bought it for
- Use it as collateral in order to borrow capital
- Pass it down to your loved ones
- Build on top of your underlying asset to create more assets

The common thread in my example? Ownership! Particularly owning capital, or owning the ability to produce an income for yourself. You're never going to earn a billion dollars pulling in a regular income from a job and paying regular income tax on it. I have yet to be proven wrong. It is actually interesting to know that, in the tax code, owning capital is more favorable than laboring for it. So, in this age when owning capital leads to wealth, laboring for it, in my opinion, is not a prudent long term strategy. I hope I am proven wrong one day because the labor force has and will always be the driving force of innovation and productivity. But in the age of automation, globalization, and financialization (the businesses of leveraging money to make more money), the opportunity to become wealthy without manual labor has shifted in favor of the owners, not the workers.

Money makes money

The term money never sleeps couldn't connect more with the notion of *owning capital*. This is because the rate of economic growth tends to trail the rate of return on capital.

- Average return on ***CAPITAL***: 5-7%

- Average growth rate of the ***ECONOMY***: 2-3%

Any inheritor of wealth or owner of capital can maintain a certain lifestyle with the income from their capital and still have their stashed capital outpacing the economy; this will always lead to a wealth and income divide in America. Working hard for "fiat" money without converting it into an economic asset that you can own is now financial suicide! It is the equivalent to holding your breath under water. You may be fine for a while, but, eventually, you will run out of air. Unfortunately, the way our system is set up, it is designed for the bearers of capital to succeed.

Can you buy an income?

Okay, so, you've made it this far! It is time to provide you with a robust investment strategy for your growing portfolio. Have you ever heard of the notion of buying cash flow? If not, welcome to the highest level of investing. This is an investment for which you don't need to network or even schmooze with a certain kind of person in order to help you get that high paying job, or speculate on the next unicorn stock to build wealth. Where you even don't have to worry about disruptive tenants or that awful HOA association leaking your profits. No, with these types of investments, all you need is money and it will make you more money without any TLC being put into it. You are welcome.

Every type of real estate has different moving parts. However, the only type of real estate that doesn't is *retail triple net* and *industrial triple net* leases. This is where cap rate really belongs. Where there are mostly no landlord responsibilities, and any expenses you have can be built into the CAM (*Common Area and Maintenance*) at the end of the year. I don't believe in a *CAP* rate when it comes to certain type of real estate, because you may have unexpected expenses that you cannot get reimbursed by the tenant for.

For example:

- If a tenant rents your apartment and leaves, you as the owner are on the hook for covering bills on top of the vacancy.
- If a tenant rents from you, they are only responsible for the guidelines of the lease. They don't have to do things to help increase the value of your property if it is not in the lease. But you, as the owner, must insure that the property is maintained, and that includes anything outside of the scope of vacancy and maintenance.

Whoever came up with cap rates for residential type housing, hotels, and mobile homes, came up with a trick to increase the value of the property they are selling you. It is almost impossible to account for all surprises when renting out your rental properties. However, with retail and industrial NNN leases, everything is paid and accounted for by the tenant and this agreement is tied into the lease. CAP rates with this type of real estate is simple. If you buy a property for $1 million dollars, and the cap rate is 5%, you will get exactly $50,000. There are no surprises; you know exactly what you get.

Triple net lease investing: NO NO NO

Welcome to the holy grail of investing in real estate. This form of investing, my friend, is for the big institutions of the world. The R.E.I.T.S, real estate moguls and other billionaire investors migrate to this in order to own a super passive investment. This is a way to be your own version of the major company Realty Income Trust (O stock). If owning the building that Amazon rents, sitting back, and collecting money off real estate, with absolutely no risk or management sounds like something you are interested in, this is the type of asset for you. Triple net lease or, or simply put, NO, NO, NO leases!

Here is how I'd buy a Net leased property. Let's say I am looking for an internet-proof retail store and I come across a KFC for $500k. You can't eat the internet, can you? I will first get the numbers on the business and the stock to see of the company is doing well. If the business is doing well, I will check how long KFC's lease is. Normal NNN leases last for 15-25 years. I would need to have at least 20% of the down payment to buy the KFC; however, if I use the bank's money, I can get a better return on my money. This is known as a *cash on cash* return.

So here is the game:

1. Go to the bank and tell them, "This property produces exactly X amount of income from a fortune 500 company tenant."

2. I have 20%, or 100k, saved for a down payment, and I want an interest only loan (make sure the loan lasts for the term of the lease). An interest only loan allows you to take advantage of more income, because you will only be paying on the *interest* and not the principle until the term is over. This is an advanced strategy, so always consult with your CPA.

3. The cap rate, if it is a really good deal, should be around 7%. This means that the income would be 7% of the purchase price of the KFC (500k), or $35,000 per year in 100% management/maintenance free income. The banks today are lending at 3-4% today, so let's use 4% to be safe. That means they will charge you 4% of the 400,000 they are going to lend you to buy that KFC at 500k.

4. This means that the banks will charge you $16k to use their money. The property is paying $35K a year to you. You deduct the income from the property 35K, from the interest $16K and this is your profit! $19,000 free and clear, every year.

5. This $19,000 on your $100,000 represents a 19% return on your money without you spending anything on maintenance, taxes, or property insurance.

This strategy provides a serious return on your money, especially when the stock market has historically only returned 6-7% annually. This is a way to safely invest and build a massive amount of wealth simultaneously. Thank me later.

Starbucks can be your next tenant

The interesting thing about Triple Net Lease investing is that, unlike stocks, you have a guarantee that the company will pay you. For example, someone can say, "Jeremiah, I really believe that Starbucks is a great company and is going to be profitable for the next 10 years." They can show you the stock price increasing over the last five years as proof, and the market would even reflect what the investor has presented. However, my question would be, "where is the Starbucks' price going next?" The stock can go down simply because of macro-economic factors such as trade wars, political issues, a recession, and the company's projected forecast, even if the stock's fundamentals are doing great. This is why I would rather be the landlord of the business than the stockholder. If I am the landlord of the property that Starbucks occupies, I don't have to worry about any dip in the stock price or government shutdown. This is because Starbucks will sign a lease saying they have to pay me a fixed amount every single month to use my land (known as a ground lease). They can even guarantee payment by using some of their business assets as collateral. So, essentially, I am both the landlord and the investor. Even if the tenant ends up going bankrupt and leaves, you still have a building that you could rent out to another fortune 500 tenant—hopefully, this time, a better one.

VIATICAL LIFE SETTLEMENT (DEATH BONDS)

Question: *How would you like to buy into an investment with 50-60% equity at an instant discount from day one!?*

You might be thinking "The only way this could happen is if you buy an undervalued, distressed property, fix it up, and flip it for a profit." But what if I told you that there was another tax free way? Allow me to introduce something called a viatical settlement, commonly referred to as a death bond.

This may be the most sinister way to garner wealth, and before we continue on, let me say that, in my opinion, this strategy is almost heinous in nature. The sad reality however, is that as morbid as this financial strategy is, it is extremely profitable and recession proof. There is a ton of upside generated by adding this simple but effective model to one's wealth strategy. The strategy is what is known as buying "death bonds," or viatical life settlements. This is created when someone has a life insurance policy and they want to get more than the cash value today, instead of waiting to perish in order to receive it. The sooner people die, the higher the yield or return, and the longer it takes, the lower the yield becomes. Now do you see why I am cringing writing this information? There are people—fund managers, insurance companies, and wealthy individuals—profiting off of this death insurance strategy. You're probably asking one of two questions, one practical, and the other opportunistic: "How can someone time the death of another person?" and "Funeral services also earn a living from death." Allow me to answer the first question. It wouldn't be a sustainable or recession resistant financial strategy if you couldn't, right? It would be a losing proposition on the investor's end, because it is hard to play God! So, to maximize the likelihood of a sufficient return, the strategy is to take on the policies of the terminally ill and the elderly. Do you see what I mean when I say it's a heinous strategy? I am going to leave my commentary out of this and continue for those who want sure ways to build wealth like the 1%. So how does this benefit the terminally ill person?

If someone, for example, is approaching death and they want to enjoy life's wonders or get more than their cash value to give to loved ones, they are more inclined to doing so. As an investor, the viatical settlement allows you to invest about $50,000 up front, plus monthly premiums, in return for a million dollar policy.

This unique and esoteric strategy is a part of the portfolios of many of the world's wealthiest people and is not disclosed to the public for many reasons. My guess is one is the upside and predictability of this strategy. So there you have it: the true definition of a million dollars' worth of game.

Your retirement accounts can purchase an island

Okay on a brighter note, there are more ways to invest at a high level if you want to avoid the dead or, in this case, the living. Land, as far back as anyone can remember, has been considered by many to be a valuable commodity, and an idea Mark Twain captured in his simple quote, "Buy land: they aren't making it anymore." His phrase couldn't be more applicable than when it comes to buying private islands. Now I know what you are thinking. How can one afford said private island earning a modest wage, with little in savings and investments? Well, believe it or not, not all islands are millions of dollars. You can, in fact, buy an island for as cheap as 500k, or the price of a condo in Brooklyn, New York, or Los Angeles. Unbelievable, right? Remember, this book is about introducing you to high level investments without breaking your bank. In that case, private islands would be considered in that high grade investment category.

Obviously, private islands are real estate and the same rule of location, location, location applies when purchasing this special property. Private islands make incredible investments for the ultra-wealthy, because no matter what happens with the world economy, whether it be a global economic meltdown or a booming economy, islands will always be a way to store capital and make the wealthy wealthier. Since buying islands are a rich person's game, in the event of needing capital, the private island can always be sold to some other wealthy liquid investor. Private islands are considered the real estate of our global economy. Prime ministers in Europe compete with Americans and the Chinese for an island in the Bahamas. It doesn't matter the nationality or geography, the wealthy of all continents knows the value of privacy and islands, and they are willing to bid up to the moon in order to get their hands on both. Islands are prime assets and, no matter what happens to our world, they will always be a considered a real asset, and serve as a getaway destination for the ultra-wealthy fleeing their countries.

So what do you need to look for when buying an island? There are myriad different factors that determine the value potential of an island; however, I would think of the following:

- ***Location, of course***: I would look at where the wealthy are buying islands and find cheap alternatives nearby. Location is a huge indicator of an island's value.
- ***Protected safe harbor***: Easy access to and from the island would have a slight impact on the value.
- ***Mainland power:*** This is power already built into the island, so you don't have to run your own power. This is also great for development opportunities.
- ***Elevation of Island:*** How high is the island elevation from the sea water? Will the island be at risk of sinking in the decades ahead? The Maldives are a great example of this one.
- ***Airstrip/ID:*** To have your own runway airstrip and *international identifier*, making it easier for pilots to locate the island, would drastically increase the value of your island.

You put all of these factors together and I believe it will come up with the perfect island for a beginner investor. Similar to buying land, an island can also be a part of your winning investment portfolio, and you would have to be a millionaire to accomplish this.

Own up the corporate balance sheet

This option is also a financial gem, hidden from popular financial advice and information. Since a BB (double B) or BBB (triple B) bond is serviced before a corporation pays a dividend on a common stock, you can own up the balance sheet of a corporation, ensuring a guaranteed payment and protection of your principal in the event of a worst-case scenario of a bankruptcy. If you own a stock that goes to zero or files for bankruptcy, you will be at risk of losing the entire principal amount plus some on your investment. Owning a corporate's bond, preferred stock, convertible, and floating rate note will allow you to avoid these perils of owning equities.

Are you an owner who wants to worry about profits every quarter? Are you constantly hoping that your stocks beat the earnings estimates, or that trade wars doesn't drag down the stock price of your investment? If you are, then a preferred stock might be for you. A preferred stock is similar to a bond in that it offers a fixed income and is interest rate sensitive. However, that is where the comparison ends. A preferred stock is like investing in the company stock without buying its shares. You just own company x, say Apple, and Apple pays you, say, a 6% of its par value for owning its preferred shares. The only problem is that this strategy is interest rate sensitive and value increases don't increase the value of a preferred stock. It's a safer income play, nothing more, nothing less. Any day rates go up, the market price will drop; whereas, if there are low interest rates, preferred stocks will tend to go up. Preferred stock is merely a dividend play that allows you to have a higher claim than stock.

If you own preferred stock, you are paid what is known as a promised income payment. That's how they keep you quiet; but if you own common stock, since you're an owner you have to receive full discloser from the company in which you are investing. The company has to report to you (and the SEC) everything that they do.

Avoid paying for college:

Want to know why the rich always win? Follow the loopholes.

Most often, the best investment strategies require no output of capital at all. Sometimes all you need is the right information. Interestingly enough, the same rules apply when it comes to paying for their children's education. Parents could legally exploit this esoteric loophole when it comes to college affordability. By giving up custody or legal guardianship of your child, they are able to claim dramatically lower incomes, qualifying the child to earn need-based financial aid.

This is how the strategy works according to AOL:

1. *During the child's junior or senior years of high school, wealthy parents file paperwork to transfer legal custody of their kids to other relatives, friends, or even co-workers.*
2. *When the transfers are complete, students are then able to declare themselves financially independent on college applications.*

In one instance detailed by the Journal, a student whose parents owned a $1.2 million home only had to declare $4,200 in income from a summer job. The process of manipulating the financial aid system, although I question its morality, is unfortunately 100 percent legal! That is right, the people earning more than $1 million dollars can pay very little to no college tuition whatsoever because of this loophole. If you fall under the average middle class income threshold of less than $80,000, you probably haven't heard of this strategy. It is not your fault; the wealthy can pay for the best advisors and accountants to share this information with them.

Sometimes the best investment is to do nothing

We've discovered that the wealthy have many investment secrets that aren't shared with the masses. From leasing property to Fortune 500 companies with no landlord responsibilities, avoiding that large tuition bill for their kids, all the way to investing in death, investors have found uncommon investments to become wealthy. However, perhaps more important than the high level investments are the investments the super wealthy don't make. The latest and greatest investment opportunity may be fun to talk about, but would-be billionaires who jump in on the "next big thing" discover that it doesn't always turn out to be so big or work out. Many of the ultra-wealthy, who make billions from their investments avoid flashy, fun, and high-risk picks and instead choose those with long-term potential to provide great returns. They watch from the sidelines as others are swept up in the frenzy of the dot-com era or the boom in cryptocurrencies. You can make and lose money in any economy. This is why having the right information and knowledge is key to succeeding with this strategy. This is why knowledge is the new money.

Wealth is something you possess, not flaunt.

Chapter 7:

JOIN THE NEW CAPITALISM

There is this polarity happening within our society that is feeding into the system of capitalism. Many people are either for or against this model, nothing in between. I can certainly understand: rolling back regulations for corporations, tax cuts for the rich, and the banking industry's financialization model of creating derivatives have all drastically contributed to the rapid wealth disparity we are currently witnessing. But is this epidemic theirs to blame 100%? I mean, after all, in a free market, it is we who give anything value. Things are merely expensive because we are willing to pay for it, often with debt, and people get away with unethical practices. This is why cars, concert tickets, and luxury items are marked up so high. A true free market in society should offer an ease of entry, lots of competition, better/ cheaper products and no bureaucracy. However, what is going on today is quite the opposite of what capitalism is supposed to be. Even billionaire Ray Dalio agrees that this current form of capitalism isn't sustainable. So why are we allowing it? I believe this all goes back to education, and nothing is more important in a capitalist society than the education of money—particularly its role in society and just how to manage and grow it.

The truth about money and capitalism

Money is overwhelmingly created and introduced to the markets through what is known as credit (debt). This credit (created out of thin air, might I add) is given out and is to be paid back with interest. The true purpose of money today is meant to be purely electronic and is worth something only because the buyer and a seller believes in it. What this means is that the financial system can issue you fake money for an asset or resources, and if you can afford to pay the money plus the interest back, you lose not only the money, but also the asset and resources. This is for no other reason than there is not enough money in circulation to pay back the debt that you owe. So, essentially, this is an organized high jacking of the real wealth of the world through the use of credit. This is how the whole machine works. It is not as complicated as many people would have you believe; it simply requires that you tap into the conscious side of capitalism in order to find out the truth. Your goal is not only to learn the game, but to own the game. Understand how money is created and use it to your advantage to acquire real assets from debt backed money that is not in your name. This is how you control capital and own your time and freedom.

Today's capitalism builds bubbles

Capitalism has been engineered to create financial bubbles. The irony of low interest rates today is that corporations can borrow billions of dollars, and instead of reinvesting it into hiring more people and innovating, what they do with the money is almost perverse. They can simply apply what is known as financial engineering. This is where they simply use the money to buy another company, or buy back stock, lay off workers, and show a better number on their bottom line because of these actions. It is almost the equivalent to an athlete taking steroids. It is a short term fix, increasing the company's multiple. Low rates are, by definition, building bubbles. When asset prices expand in order to meet the low interest rates expansion of currency, this forces the little guy to invest in high risk assets to get a yield on their money. If low interest rates were as simple as a panacea, then there wouldn't be conscious recessions and drastic corrections in the market. Where do you draw the line in the structural element of capitalism, the financial engineering that forces risk and creates bubbles? My guess is people will begin rushing to the exit in droves once the rates begin to increase or once the game of financial musical chairs ends. Deja vu seems to be a common theme in capitalism.

Capitalism needs guardrails

Capitalism's name seems to be tarnished. As an entrepreneur, you should be thinking about building sustainable systems, not just flipping and living off of the buying and selling of others. The main focus in capitalism has always been about building, innovation, and trading value. That was until the rise of financialization and the emergence of managerial capitalism begun in the late 1970s. Managerial capitalists control other people's money and budget and have borrowed power and influence. There is a difference between a managerial capitalist and an entrepreneur (an actual capitalist), but they both somehow get looped in together.

Sadly, most people today do not understand the difference between being a true capitalist and being a managerial capitalist. C-suite executives and CEOs are often seen by the media as the modern-day capitalists of our society. However, I believe this is far from the truth. Many of these people have been guilty of being takers, selfish, and often greedy. This is shown when CEOs pay themselves huge bonuses while cutting thousands of jobs within their workforce. This is also exhibited through stock buyback. Stock buyback is when a CEO borrows money from the banks (usually during lower interest rates) and uses the funds to buy back company stock to increase the stock price. Instead of creating more jobs or investing in R&D that will help the business grow, the CEOs increase the stock price, allowing them to grow their wealth. Is this the result of the knowledge taught in business schools and MBA programs? Are they teaching our students the nature of greed and the "profit over anything" mentality? Or are they teaching them how to build sustainable companies, become givers, and create value for others?

> *"How to equip a generation of Americans for success in entrepreneurship? Forget about MBAs. Most business schools teach you how to be successful in big corporations rather than start your own company. But starting something from scratch and maturing it as it grows is where our country has been at its strongest and most innovative."*
>
> \- Dr. Frank Luntz

Entrepreneurs, our true capitalists, are the pillars of civilization, and we need more of these kinds of capitalists in our communities. These types of people put up their own money, take huge risks, spearhead innovation, and create jobs for others. They are the givers of modern society, and we should appreciate and applaud them, no matter their economic position in our community.

Conscious capitalism is not about greed

In capitalism, the desire to get rich quick has historically been the quintessential and surest way for the masses to lose money. On the other hand, ironically, that same desire has allowed the wealthy to take advantage of this social economic emotion. For example:

- Let's say you have $500, and you want to make 20% in a year; say $100 dollars. Is making $100 profit exciting or engaging enough for an average retail investor?

To the majority, it will not be as exciting as making $1000 from the $500 initial investment. This philosophy has been a huge problem for the poor and middle class and a huge opportunity for the wealthy and financially literate. The constant social reinforcement of 'more is better' has created a culture of takers. True capitalism, in my opinion, is having empathy and being a giver. The ability to empathize with the masses and create value not only for oneself but for others. Real capitalists do not need to attend an MBA program to become successful. In fact, the best education one can receive is real-world stimulation and experience. This type of education is priceless, comes with failure, and requires a ton of selflessness and empathy. Rather than knowing how to spend money like a managerial capitalist, real capitalists know how to create and make money from nothing. They are the reasons corporations are established in the first place and why managerial capitalists even have jobs. Without real capitalism and entrepreneurship, there would be no jobs, innovation, or productivity within our society.

Watch out for 'The Joneses'

Have you ever wondered how all your friends, whether on social media or in real life, are able to afford all that they are doing? You know, the house, the car, the jewelry, the vacations? The odds are very high that they can't afford It. More than 70 percent of Americans live paycheck to paycheck and that cuts across income spectrums. Yes, that is right: 70%! I have personally met people who can save on incomes of $25,000 a year, and people who don't have a penny in savings on salaries of $250,000+ a year. The harsh truth, unfortunately, is most Americans don't live within their means. This competitive consumerism culture of trying to keep up with the neighbor has been the only tool used to keep the masses blind to the truth. Who is benefiting from this race to the financial slaughterhouse? Introducing one of the top 5 billionaires in the world, one whom many consumers don't even know, Bernald Arnault, the founder and CEO of LVMH, one of the most prestige luxury brands in the world. It is certainly not his fault that he makes an average of $2.2

billion a day and is worth over $99 billion, more than the state of Hawaii. This notion forced me to step back to see things through a different lens. Think about how much of your money has been quietly siphoned back to the rich by your uncontrollable consumption of high-end items like Gucci, Louis Viton, Birkin bags, and Mercedes Benz. Now ask yourself, "Is my appetite to spend money driven by the media or public perception, or is it really due to low self-esteem?" Now, I understand that the media, advertisement companies, and public perception make this task of delayed gratification a difficult one to accomplish, but in doing this you will set yourself free mentally and financially. The trick is to stay as far away from the Joneses as possible and focus on building your last name. This keeps you from the temptation of the fear of missing out and, instead, allows you to re-shift the focus on what truly matters.

Golden handcuffs

Capitalism has also found a way to subtly and stealthily exploit the economic energy of laborers and workers. And nothing is more insidious than the pervasive corporate financial allure. This financial allure that corporations use is a robust psychological tool used to keep employees motivated enough to work, but honest enough to stay at their job. Even if the thought of leaving seems appealing to the employee, these financial incentives serve as a golden handcuff to prevent one from leaving a company. Welcome to the main ingredient of financial persuasion that allows the CEO to get away with earning 30 times what the average employee makes, and for less work.

Golden handcuffs were first introduced in 1976 as a corporate strategy to keep their highest performing, but unhappy workers. These employees were paid so extremely well, given their level of experience and industry options, that it discouraged an employee from taking employment elsewhere. Ever heard of a company vesting schedule? In a way these programs are a way for a company to dangle the financial carrot in the hope that employees continue to chase it. The notion that you have a set amount of cash waiting for you if you work a number of years is a sure way to keep anyone who is economically deprived committed to laboring for the corporation. It seems like a glamourous form of servitude, if you ask me. However, this trick is one of the many reasons why controlled capitalism exists. Why would someone bother to challenge the enormous wealth disparity between CEOs and employees, or even leave a company, when you will leave money on the table in doing so? These golden handcuffs, whether you refer to them as stock option, vesting, corporate incentives, or free money, are an insidious tax on one's time, options, and more importantly, one's happiness. Once again, capitalism wins because of micro financial implementations such as these.

Audacity separates the haves from the have nots

Not only do schools teach us about only one way to earn an income (working a job), but they charge us (usually through debt) for it. The irony is, it is not until you are out of a job or owe your alma mater over 100k that you are introduced to the "rich man's income." The good news is that, once you start producing the rich man's income, which happens to be portfolio and passive income, you will pay less in taxes, have more time, and produce more value!

This seems like something worth pursuing, even with an education, degree, or a comfortable high paying job, right? But how do you get to the rich man's income? Especially if you have no money, no education credentials, experience, or family fortune? You must have the audacity to pursue it.

Remember this. Audacity is only viewed as a negative to the bearer of the object you're aiming to pursue. In other words, "who are you to demand this from me?" The biggest marketing play to keep the dollar circulating in the hands of the 1% and .01% has been the idea that fortune favors the socially fittest and most intellectually apt to survive. This ploy has been more psychological than it has been physical. The thought that you need to go to the best schools in order to land a high paying job or gain wealth, sign a deal with a publishing company in order to write a book, know top investors from Silicon Valley in order to get funding for your startup, and have years of experience in any industry in order to branch off and start your own business, has kept many from unlocking their hidden gifts and potential. The truth is, we all possess a certain genius-level skill or talent that allows us to bypass ubiquitous social steps and achieve our goals at lightning speed. Sure, there will be resistance and obstacles along the way, as we are not immune to any of that. However, having the audacity to do often separates the haves from the have nots. When you display the audacity to do something, you are intrinsically saying to the universe that you believe and are confident in the path that is already set for you.

Audacity, for lack of a better word, is hope. And hope is so strong, you only need five percent of it to change your life! The audacity to do is derived from ambition, determination, aspiration, and faith; all important signs of having hope. Audacity is a simple understanding that where you are today will not determine where you will be tomorrow. Audacity enables you to take back the power of your circumstances and gain control of your destiny. This simple choice of having the audacity to do something can change your entire trajectory in life, even if the changes are subtle.

Join the new capitalism of giving

There are enough resources in the world to go around. However, we have been conditioned to think and move as though these resources are limited. The ultimate goal is to teach you how to fish so that you can establish your independence and operate out of abundance rather than fear and greed. I am releasing all of the information that has been stealthily and strategically kept from the masses because I want to create a new wave of financially savvy and educated people. These people will not only be financially equipped on a mental level but display a kind of empathy that will enable them to share their knowledge with someone less fortunate than they are. I believe this is the genuine meaning of social Darwinism. Social Darwinism is a theory put forward by Herbert spencer. The theory became a social construct to justify manufactured and systematic ways to survive. This antiquated theory needs a reboot. It should no longer be about the survival of the fittest individual. It should be about the survival of the most suitable humanity. We all need to learn to share our secrets if we want humanity to survive and thrive for millennia to come. Otherwise, we will continue this process of single elimination until there is no one else to eliminate, and humanity as a whole will cease to exist.

HAS ANYTHING CHANGED IN THE LAST 30 YEARS?

"The richest one percent of this country owns half our country's wealth, five trillion dollars. One third of that comes from hard work, two thirds comes from inheritance, interest on interest accumulating to widows and idiot sons and what I do, stock and real estate speculation. It's bullshit. You got ninety percent of the American public out there with little or no net worth. I create nothing. I own. We make the rules, pal. The news, war, peace, famine, upheaval, the price per paper clip. We pick that rabbit out of the hat while everybody sits out there wondering how the hell we did it. Now you're not naive enough to think we're living in a democracy, are you buddy? It's the free market. And you're a part of it. You've got that killer instinct. Stick around pal, I've still got a lot to teach you."

—Gorden Gekko, 1987

YOU DECIDE...

Meet the author...

Jeremiah J. Brown is an entrepreneur, investor, and best-selling author of three books. Even before the age of 30, he achieved success with multiple business ventures. He has been featured in various publications, including Cheddar, Ebony Magazine, Respect, Newsweek, Billboard, and Entrepreneur Magazine. Brown's entrepreneurship has allowed him to become an investor—an investor in people, and in the education of those who desire to be financially free.

Dedication

Family can be defined in many ways. I define family as a group of people united by certain convictions or a common fellowship. This book is dedicated to the people whom I call family. You, the reader, are now a part of my tribe, my family, and I am grateful for your support. This book is also dedicated to the women who have inspired me, Sydney D. Brown, Angela Vega, and Anne Connors! You are reading this book because of them. They all understand the impact that financial literacy has in shifting a culture, and they gave me the grace and support to share my knowledge with the world. With over 55 thousand copies of my books sold to date, I am more than grateful to have them by my side physically and in spirit. I love you all.

In living memory...
Anne Connors (My Teacher)

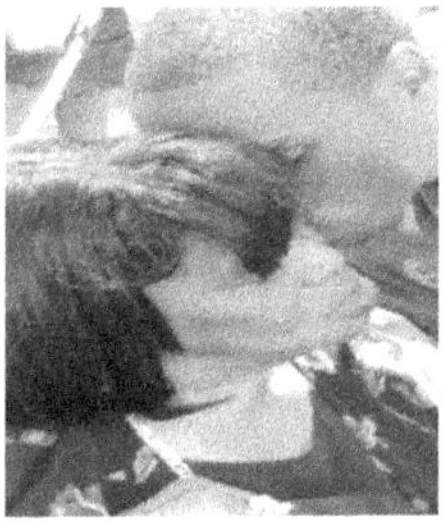

And when great souls die,
after a period peace blooms,
slowly and always
irregularly. Spaces fill
with a kind of
soothing electric vibration.
Our senses, restored, never
to be the same, whisper to us.
They existed. They existed.
We can be. Be and be
better. For they existed."

– Maya Angelou

An educated mind cannot be enslaved.

CPSIA information can be obtained
at www.ICGtesting.com
Printed in the USA
LVHW111424270120
644907LV00001B/1/J

9 780578 562018